The Revolutionary War

by Gail B. Stewart

Lucent Books, P.O. Box 289011, San Diego, CA 92198-9011

Books in the America's Wars Series:

The Revolutionary War
The Indian Wars
The War of 1812
The Mexican-American War
The Civil War
The Spanish-American War

World War I
World War II: The War in the Pacific
World War II: The War in Europe
The Korean War
The Vietnam War
The Persian Gulf War

Library of Congress Cataloging-in-Publication Data

Stewart, Gail, 1949–
    The Revolutionary War / by Gail Stewart.
       p. cm — (America's wars)
    Includes bibliographical references and index.
    Summary: Examines the causes, events, and aftermath of the conflict that has been called "America's first civil war."
    ISBN 1-56006-400-5
    1. United States—History—Revolution, 1775–1783—Juvenile literature. [1. United States—History—Revolution, 1775–1783.]
I. Title. II. Series
E208.S86   1991   91-29889
973.3—dc20

Contents

Foreword

War, justifiable or not, is a descent into madness. George Washington, America's first president and commander-in-chief of its armed forces, wrote that his most fervent wish was "to see this plague of mankind, war, banished from the earth." Most, if not all of the forty presidents who succeeded Washington have echoed similar sentiments. Despite this, not one generation of Americans since the founding of the republic has been spared the maelstrom of war. In its brief history of just over two hundred years, the United States has been a combatant in eleven major wars. And four of those conflicts have occurred in the last fifty years.

America's reasons for going to war have differed little from those of most nations. Political, social, and economic forces were at work which either singly or in combination ushered America into each of its wars. A desire for independence motivated the Revolutionary War. The fear of annihilation led to the War of 1812. A related fear, that of having the nation divided, precipitated the Civil War. The need to contain an aggressor nation brought the United States into the Korean War. And territorial ambition lay behind the Mexican-American and the Indian Wars. Like all countries, America, at different times in its history, has been victimized by these forces and its citizens have been called to arms.

Whatever reasons may have been given to justify the use of military force, not all of America's wars have been popular. From the Revolutionary War to the Vietnam War, support of the people has alternately waxed and waned. For example, less than half of the colonists backed America's war of independence. In fact, most historians agree that at least one-third were committed to maintaining America's colonial status. During the Spanish-American War, a strong antiwar movement also developed. Resistance to the war was so high that the Democratic party made condemning the war a significant part of its platform in an attempt to lure voters into voting Democratic. The platform stated that "the burning issue of imperialism growing out of the Spanish war involves the very existence of the Republic and the destruction of our free institutions." More recently, the Vietnam War divided the nation like no other conflict had since the Civil War. The mushrooming antiwar movements in most major cities and colleges throughout the United States did more to bring that war to a conclusion than did actions on the battlefield.

Yet, there have been wars which have enjoyed overwhelming public support. World Wars I and II were popular because people believed that the survival of America's democratic institutions was at stake. In both wars, the American people rallied with an enthusiasm and spirit of self-sacrifice that was remarkable for a country with such a diverse population. Support for food and fuel rationing, the purchase of war bonds, a high rate of voluntary enlistments, and countless other forms of voluntarism, were characteristic of the people's response to those wars. Most recently, the Persian Gulf War prompted an unprecedented show of support even though the United States was not directly threatened by the conflict. Rallies in support of U.S. troops were widespread. Tens of thousands of individuals, including families, friends, and well-wishers of the troops sent packages of food, cosmetics, clothes, cassettes, and suntan oil. And even more supporters wrote letters to unknown soldiers that were forwarded to the military front. In fact, most public opinion polls revealed that up to 90 percent of all Americans approved of their nation's involvement.

The complex interplay of events and purposes that leads to military conflict should be included in a history of any war. A simple chronicling of battles and casualty lists at best offers only a partial history of war. Wars do not spontaneously erupt; nor does their memory perish. They are driven by underlying causes, fueled by policymakers, fought and supported by citizens, and remembered by those plotting a nation's future. For these reasons wars, or the fear of wars, will always leave an indelible stamp on any nation's history and influence its future.

The purpose of this series is to provide a full understanding of America's Wars by presenting each war in a historical context. Each of the twelve volumes focuses on the events that led up to the war, the war itself, its impact on the home front, and its aftermath and influence upon future conflicts. The unique personalities, the dramatic acts of courage and compassion, as well as the despair and horror of war are all presented in this series. Together, they show why America's wars have dominated American consciousness in the past as well as how they guide many political decisions of today. In these vivid and objective accounts, students will gain an understanding of why America became involved in these conflicts, and how historians, military and government officials, and others have come to understand and interpret that involvement.

Chronology of Events

1763

The end of the French and Indian War; also, Britain's King George issues proclamation to the American colonies forbidding westward expansion.

1765

Parliament passes the Stamp Act.

1770

March 5   Five colonists die in what came to be known as the Boston Massacre, a street argument that got out of control.

1773

December 16   The Boston Tea Party is held in Boston Harbor as a rebellion against the Tea Act.

1774

Parliament passes the Intolerable Acts.

September 5   The first Continental Congress meets in Philadelphia to protest the Intolerable Acts.

1775

April 19   British and American troops clash in Lexington and Concord.

June 17   The Battle of Breed's Hill is fought, the bloodiest of the entire war.

July 3   Washington takes control of the Continental army.

1776

July 4   The Declaration of Independence is signed by members of the Continental Congress.

August 17   German mercenaries (Hessians) arrive in New York to fight for the British.

August 27   British defeat the American army at New York's Long Island; this begins the war-long occupation of New York City by the British.

December 26   Washington's troops surprise the Hessians, defeating them in the Battle of Trenton.

1777

October 17   A large portion of the British army surrenders at Saratoga, New York.

December 19   Washington leads his troops to miserable winter quarters at Valley Forge.

1778

February 6   France and America sign an alliance.

November 11   Butler's Rangers, aided by Mohawk chief Joseph Brant, massacre settlers at Cherry Valley, New York.

December 29   British capture Savannah, Georgia.

1779

February 24   George Rogers Clark and his small band of men capture the British fort at Vincennes on the Wabash River, and "Hair Buyer" Hamilton is sent to prison.

September 23   John Paul Jones's ship *Bonhomme Richard* captures the British ship *Serapis* in a bloody sea battle.

1780

May 12   The city of Charleston, South Carolina, falls into British control.

October 7   Over-mountain men soundly defeat British and Loyalist troops at King's Mountain, North Carolina.

1781

April 25   British general Cornwallis begins his campaign to end the war quickly by taking Virginia.

August 14   Washington, hearing French admiral de Grasse is coming to Chesapeake Bay with a large naval force, makes plans to secretly send his army to Yorktown.

October 19   Cornwallis surrenders at Yorktown, ending the British military threat in America.

1783

America and Great Britain officially end the war by signing a peace treaty in Paris.

INTRODUCTION

The World Turned Upside Down

It was a muggy, overcast morning in Yorktown, Virginia—unseasonably warm for October 17, 1781. A battle had been raging between British and American forces. The booming of cannons was deafening.

At about ten o'clock that morning, a few soldiers on the American side began shouting. Activity was taking place beyond the large hill the soldiers called "Horn Work." They could see a swatch of red cloth and wondered if the British were beginning an attack.

But the red cloth was the coat of a single small British soldier. He was a drummer, a regular member of armies in the eighteenth century. He wore the same scarlet coat and bearskin hat as the soldiers. But his pants, wound tight around his short, skinny legs, showed him to be only a boy. He was too young and too small to be a soldier leading a charge.

The boy climbed quickly to the top of the hill. He stood tall and began to beat out a long, continuous drum roll.

At first, no one heard the sound through the rattling of gunfire and the crashing of the big guns. All they could see was his pale, frightened face and his sticks hitting the skin of the drum. Years later, Americans who were there would remember that the boy looked ghostly, like a vision in the swirling clouds of mist and smoke.

After a few minutes, the rest of the American army did notice him. One by one, the guns stopped firing, and the soldiers sat quietly and listened.

The British army had sent out the lone drummer because its commanders wished to have a parley, or conference. That morning, the British commander Lord Cornwallis was ready to surrender. One American lieutenant wrote in his journal that he had "never heard a drum equal to it—the most delightful music to us all!"

The drummer boy was followed by a British officer waving a white handkerchief to signal the surrender. He was blindfolded by the Americans and taken off to Gen. George Washington's headquarters. There he would meet with Washington and discuss terms for the war's end. After six long years, the Revolutionary War was over.

"If Ponies Rode Men and Grass Ate Cows"

In the afternoon of October 19, a special ceremony marked the surrender of the British troops. The victorious American troops stood at attention in two lines. British soldiers marched between the lines.

As was the custom, the defeated army demonstrated that they were no longer a threat. The British soldiers walked with their flags rolled up so that the colors were not visible. In another gesture of submission, they carried unloaded muskets without the razor-sharp bayonets attached. At a given signal from their commander, the British soldiers were to place their empty weapons in a pile.

American soldiers later remembered that the British troops were clearly unhappy. Many soldiers' eyes were red and swollen from crying. "They were ashamed, it appeared to us," wrote one corporal. "Their lines were broken and ragged, and they weren't a-stepping together. We knew they were wondering how they might have been defeated by an army like ours."

Many of the British soldiers placed their weapons down angrily, according to Dr. Joseph Thatcher, an American who was present at the ceremony.

"Some of the platoon officers appeared to be exceedingly chagrined when giving the word, 'Ground arms,' and I am a witness that they performed this duty in a very unofficerlike manner," wrote Thatcher in his military journal. "Many of the soldiers manifested a sullen temper, throwing their arms on the pile with violence, as if determined to render them useless."

The most memorable part of the ceremony, however, was the tune played by the British army band. In a ceremony such as this, the defeated army's band usually would play a military march honoring the victors. However, on this day the British band played not a military tune, but a popular song of the day called "The World Turned Upside Down."

> If ponies rode men and if grass ate cows,
> And cats should be chased into holes by the mouse,
> If summers were spring and the other way round,
> Then all the world would be upside down.

The British surrender their arms to General Washington in 1781.

The choice of this particular tune surprised many who were there. But the tune was certainly appropriate. The highly trained British army had been defeated by a ragtag bunch of Continental soldiers. The world really had turned upside down.

A War Like No Other

It is easy to understand why many of the British soldiers felt ashamed when they had to surrender to the Americans. This was certainly not a war that the British expected to lose.

In the 1700s, Britain's power was undisputed. It had a mighty army and the greatest navy on earth. Although such terms were not used in the eighteenth century, it would today be classified as a superpower.

America, on the other hand, was nothing—at least as far as military might was concerned. It was an assortment of individual colonies which, until war broke out, had never had to work together. With a population of only 2.5 million, the American colonies did not even have an army. At the start of the war, not only had the British doubted whether the Americans would dare to fight the "Mother Country," many were confident that if war did break out, Britain would defeat the colonists in a matter of weeks. But the British were wrong. The Americans did fight, and with such tenacity that the war lasted for six long years.

Stern Men in White Wigs

For many people, the Revolutionary War seems dull and uninteresting. The events seem to be so distant and remote that it's difficult to take interest in the men with white wigs and formal bearing. While people recognize many of the important historical figures, the details of the war itself seem unimportant. What was the war really like? It was *not* dominated by the famous people in history books, such as George Washington and Benjamin Franklin. The story of the American Revolution is a story of ordinary people who lived through some very extraordinary circumstances. It was a time of great risk. The stakes were high; the British would have hanged any Americans who participated in the fight, had they lost.

The Revolutionary War was fought on many fronts. Famous battles were fought in Philadelphia, New York, and Boston. But battles were fought in the American South, too. The war took place at sea, as well, in violent clashes between British and American ships. And some of the most vicious fighting took place between Native Americans and American settlers on the frontier.

The war was also a clashing, overt, bloody war, full of unbelievable cruelty. Of course, every war is violent—that is the nature of war. But this was a time of hand-to-hand combat, with bayonets, hatchets, knives, and fists used as often as muskets were. Witnesses to such battles said later that they were haunted by scenes of "unidentifiable pieces of bodies, men's and children's, strewn across the fields of battle."

Those soldiers killed in battle were perhaps better off than those captured by the enemy. Many prisoners were tortured into revealing battle secrets, and the methods of torture were almost beyond belief. Those "lucky" enough to be simply imprisoned were at risk, too. In fact, more American soldiers died on British prison ships than were lost in all of the military battles planned by George Washington.

Most importantly, the American Revolution was more than a war between Britain and the American colonies. Historians agree that it was really America's first civil war. There were just as many Americans loyal to the British crown as dared to defy it. The disagreements over loyalty caused hard feelings between friends and neighbors, often splitting American familes into enemy camps.

But for all the horror it brought to the people of America, the war was a first. Never before had a colony demanded its freedom and achieved it. To the men and women who dared to stand up to the British crown, being free was important enough to suffer and die for.

"The idea of independence was an impulse that could not be denied," historian Sheldon Sharritt remarked. "No other colony had ever—ever—risen up against such a great power and come away victorious. The Americans taught the world something terribly valuable."

How did this "undeniable impulse" come to be? What were the forces that changed ordinary people into revolutionaries? Why did the world turn upside down?

CHAPTER ONE

"A Gradual Disharmony"

The war that would make America independent of Britain did not start quickly. There was no single event that changed peaceful times into times of war.

Philadelphian Josiah Taylor, like many men of his day, kept a journal during the war years. In 1799, he reflected on the reasons for the war, comparing Britain and America to musical instruments.

> Perhaps we began in tune; perhaps there was favor and grace between the colonies and the Crown in the beginning. But through the years we experienced a gradual disharmony, each side becoming more and more out of tune. The music of politics between our two countries became unpleasant, and distressing to the ear.

A War Debt

This "gradual disharmony" really began after another war that ended in 1763. It was called the Seven Years' War by the British; the Americans called it the French and Indian War.

The British and the French had been struggling for almost a century over the control of North America. Their conflict erupted into war, with the American colonists siding with the British against the French and their Native American allies.

The war was long and fierce, and in the end Britain won. The French were forced to give up their large colonial holdings in North America, especially those in Canada, to the British. These new lands, added to their already huge territories around the world, made Britain the number one power in the world.

But simply owning land does not guarantee political or military strength. The war had been expensive for the British. Even though the fighting units were mainly composed of American colonists, many British army units had directed the war. Britain had paid for these soldiers—their upkeep, food, and equipment. The British had also supplied vast quantities of costly weapons and ammunition.

The need for war supplies and equipment employed a great many people in England. Ships had to be built, uniforms sewn, weapons and ammunition made. Although the British people were taxed heavily to pay for the war, at least many had jobs.

But most of these jobs ended when the war did. As a result of these expenses, Britain's national debt doubled, rising to today's equivalent of $30 billion. The economy of this eighteenth century superpower was in poor shape.

And Britain's people were suffering. Unemployment skyrocketed. Those who had been marginally poor before became destitute. Homeless families wandered the city streets; scrawny orphans begged on every corner for a crust of bread. Hungry crowds of people rioted in the streets of London demanding jobs, money, or simply a meal for their families.

American colonist Benjamin Franklin, who was working in London after the French and Indian War, said that he witnessed "riots about corn, riots about elections, riots of colliers [coal miners], riots of coal-heavers, riots of sawyers [lumbermen], riots of government chairmen, riots of smugglers."

Better Times in the Colonies

In contrast, Britain's American colonies were far removed from the troubles three thousand miles across the Atlantic Ocean. In fact, the colonies had come through the French and Indian War stronger economically than Britain. The colonies were prosperous, busy, and thriving. The backbone of the American economy was agriculture. Most of America's 2.5 million people were farmers. (One-half million of America's population were African slaves, brought to work on the farms.) Cotton, tobacco, corn, wheat, and rice were grown and sold to a ready market in England.

The fishing industry, especially in the cold waters off the Massachusetts coast, was growing, too. In addition, there was a demand for the lumber the large American forests produced. And in the fashionable stores of Europe, there was a great cry for American furs. The trappers working the American mountain wilderness had no trouble selling their pelts.

Although most colonists lived on farms, cities were growing, too. Philadelphia was the largest, with a population of forty thousand. New York, Boston, and Charleston, South Carolina, were also thriving. In colonial times, all the important towns and cities were located on the seacoast because all trade was done by ship. City dwellers made good livings from fishing, trading, and shipbuilding.

So while the British rioted and complained about the harshness of life, the Americans were satisfied. Certainly in 1763, there was no public cry to separate from Britain. Historian Allan Traynor said early colonial Americans possessed "a quiet confidence that all was right with the world. They belonged to Britain, and felt no animosity about the arrangement. On the contrary, most colonists had great faith in the lives they led."

Governing the Colonies

There were problems, of course. Many of the problems in the thirteen colonies stemmed from their being just that—thirteen separately run colonies. Each colony had its own assembly, usually called a House of Burgesses. The assemblies' representatives were elected by the registered voters in the colony, all of whom were men who had to own property to be allowed to vote. Assembly members voted on special issues, often levying taxes if there was a need. Each colony had a governor, too. These men (women were not allowed to hold such offices) were not elected; rather, they were appointed by the king. So even though each colony had an assembly, none was independent. The British lawmaking body, Parliament, had a fair amount of control over the governments and economies of the colonies.

One good example of the British hold over the colonies was the acts of trade and navigation. These laws controlled the trading and sale of goods to and by the colonies. American farmers could sell products only to Britain, even though another nation might be willing to offer a better price. The acts also prevented American manufacturers from producing any goods that might compete with British goods.

A third restriction required by the acts was imposed on imported goods. Americans could buy products not produced in England only from British ships that delivered them to the colonies. The British would heavily tax these foreign goods. These restrictions ensured that Britain would make a healthy profit from the colonies it owned.

Most Americans were not bothered by these laws because they did their best to outsmart them. Smuggling was big business. Dutch, French, Spanish, and even American ships illegally brought in goods from around the world to American ports. The same smugglers would then reload their ships with illegal American goods and sell them at foreign ports. Since no taxes were paid on these smuggled goods, the colonists benefited greatly from the activity.

Of course, smugglers faced prison—and often public hanging—if caught. But there were hundreds of miles of coastline

"Spit and Polish"

Being a good soldier in the British army meant more than fighting well. Appearance was as important to the officers in charge as skill with a bayonet and musket.

A redcoat's uniform was designed for looks, not for comfort. There was only one uniform, and it had to be worn in all seasons. The coats were made of hot, thick wool. It might have felt good on December days, but in July in New England, it was a nightmare.

The scarlet coat was decorated with linings, brass or pewter buttons, emblems, and lace, all of which added to its weight. Under the coat, each soldier wore a vest, or waistcoat, of either white or red linen depending on which regiment he was in. The coat's collar was stiff leather, designed to force the soldier to stand ramrod-straight. The collar made it painful for a soldier to move his head to the right or left and chafed against his neck, leaving bloody, raw patches.

The redcoats wore white knee britches, which had to be put on wet because they were so tight. When the pants dried, they shrank and were tighter than before. Soldiers with thin legs had no problems with the pants, but soldiers with stockier legs sometimes lost circulation in them.

Each soldier wore two belts crisscrossing his chest—one for his cartridge belt, the other for his bayonet. His pack of supplies, weighing over 135 pounds, was strapped to his back and was carried even in battle.

British redcoats wore heavy helmets made either of brass or bearskin. The helmets had no brims so were useless against the sun. It was believed by British officers that the more uncomfortable the soldiers were, the madder and more aggressively they would fight.

Each soldier was required to wear his hair in a tight ponytail. Two curls, one by each ear, were also required. These curls were held in place with a mixture of white powder and grease. Because hair was seldom washed, soldiers were plagued with smelly, dirty hair. Flies, attracted by the grease, swarmed around their heads.

British soldiers worked hard each day getting ready for inspection. Buttons had to be polished, boots blackened, hair braided and curled. Historians say redcoats worked at it for three hours a day.

along the eastern colonies, and British ships could not patrol them all. Even though the British navy was the best in the world, the smugglers could usually outfox it.

American colonists, then, did not feel the need to rebel against Britain. They were more prosperous than citizens of any other European nation. They lived in a land of bountiful resources, where their lives were rich with promise. "I love this place," wrote Rhode Island colonist Andrew Peyton to his brother in England in 1762. "I am confident of my future, not just of my fortune. I know not whether I will be wealthy, but…as an Englishman I am immensely joyful to be here."

The Proclamation of 1763

The gradual disharmony between Britain and her American colonies to which Josiah Taylor referred began shortly after the French and Indian War. A new king had come to the throne in 1760, George III. King George worried about the thirteen American colonies. He was especially concerned about the strong westward movement of American settlers across the Allegheny Mountains from Virginia, Pennsylvania, and Maryland. Native Americans were resentful about settlers moving into their lands. And the British government did not want to fight another expensive war—this time with the Indians.

To tackle the Indian problem, King George issued a proclamation in 1763. He warned the colonists that they were no longer allowed to push across the Allegheny Mountains. He ordered any settlers who had already moved into the frontier west of the Alleghenies to return to wherever they came from.

The proclamation was unpopular. People felt that it should be their decision if they wanted to move westward and take a chance on hostile Indians. How could a king thousands of miles away make that determination for them?

A "Stamp" of Disapproval

In addition to the unpopular proclamation, King George enacted other policies that angered the colonists. Still worried that the French might try to return to North America, King George decided to send ten thousand British troops to America. They would serve as a warning to any French who might be tempted to resume the fight.

The king and Prime Minister George Grenville believed the colonies should pay for the military force. Since the colonies would be the ones who would most benefit from a British peacekeeping force in North America, they should be willing to foot the bill. Salaries, supplies, and other expenses should be paid for by the colonists.

King George III wanted to prevent British colonists from moving west into Indian territory. To prevent this, he issued the Proclamation of 1763.

With the passage of the Stamp Act, a British stamp such as this one had to appear on newspapers, bills of sale, wills, diplomas, and other official documents.

To raise the money, Parliament passed the Stamp Act of 1765. The Stamp Act was the idea of Prime Minister Grenville. He devised a special seal, or stamp. Stamps were required on any official document, diploma, newspaper, will, or bill of sale. Stamps were also required on decks of playing cards and dice. Before such items were sold, American merchants were required to purchase stamps from an official stamp agent and affix them to their goods. If they did not, the merchants faced stiff fines or imprisonment. And because the stamps cost money, the merchants had to raise the costs of their goods to recoup the cost of the stamps. Grenville believed it was a marvelous idea because it hit all classes of people. It would be hard for any colonist to avoid having to purchase a stamped item—if not just on his or her weekly newspaper. As British officials like George Grenville were praising the act, American colonists were fuming.

"This is robbery, plain to see," wrote a Boston merchant in his journal. "There is no reason in Creation why [King George] must take money from our pockets only to line his own. And what say we? Who consults us on the dreaded thing?"

The Boston merchant's argument was echoed by others. The colonists' main objection to the Stamp Act was that they were being taxed without being consulted. No representative of Massachusetts, or Virginia, or of any of the other eleven colonies had been included in the sessions of Parliament when the Stamp Act was passed.

In fact, some lawmakers in the colonies stated that they would have been willing to donate money for the British army's stay. But to be taxed by Parliament—an assembly that was not their own—was a slap in the face.

Even some British officials were outraged. William Pitt, a respected member of Parliament, criticized the Stamp Act. He applauded the Americans and said:

> [The Americans] have been wronged. They have been driven to madness by injustice.... I will beg leave to tell the House what is really my opinion. It is that the Stamp Act be repealed absolutely, totally, and immediately; that the reason for the repeal should be assigned, because it was founded on an erroneous principle.

Resisting with Results

There were angry shouts of protest from many colonists after the passage of the Stamp Act. Some of the protest was peaceful, with representatives from nine of the colonies meeting in New York to draw up a formal denouncement.

Other colonists advocated boycotting British goods as a method of protest. By not buying products made in Britain or

Tar and Feathers

The patriots despised Americans loyal to the British government. Many Loyalists who spoke out in favor of the Stamp Act, or the tax on tea, or any of the other actions against the patriots were made to endure a painful punishment called Tar and Feathers. (It was not invented by the patriots; kings used it in medieval times to force people to confess to crimes.)

Being tarred and feathered was a public spectacle meant to frighten other Loyalists. The tar was melted down to a boiling, smelly ooze. As the pungent-smelling tar bubbled in the pot, the victim was made to strip down to his waist, or sometimes even completely.

Several patriots would hold him down while the boiling tar was spread over his body. Ladles were used, or even mops. As the victim screamed with pain, feather pillows were broken apart, and the feathers were scattered on his body.

Removing the tar once it cooled was supposed to be even more painful than the application. Often whole strips of skin came off with the tar, leading to infections and shock. There are recorded cases of tar-and-feather victims dying of pain or going insane from the ordeal.

After a few victims had been tarred and feathered, patriots soon found that merely the threat of the punishment was scary enough to make other Loyalists in town disappear.

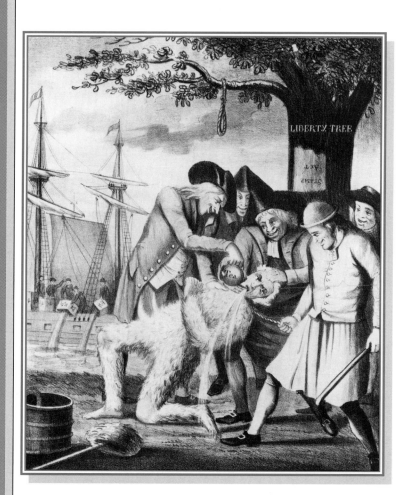

Bostonians tar and feather a British tax official. Although portrayed humorously, tarring and feathering was extremely painful for the victim.

sold by British merchants, the colonists could pressure the British economy. And if the economy suffered, the British government might give in to popular pressure and cancel the Stamp Act.

There were also more violent protestations of the Stamp Act. A number of underground organizations with names like The Liberty Boys and the Sons of Liberty sprang up, especially in cities like Boston and Philadelphia. The Sons of Liberty were young men organized by merchants, businessmen, lawyers, journalists, and others who would be most hurt by the Stamp Act. The societies communicated with each other through correspondence, supported a boycott of British goods, and incited destruction of stamped paper and violence against British officials.

The Sons made it their business to intimidate those whose job it was to sell the stamps to the colonists. They threw rocks through stamp distributors' windows or even tried to frighten the distributors by publicly hanging dummies emblazoned with the words Stamp Man. Sometimes mock funerals were held, burying dummies marked Liberty. In some cases, the Sons of Liberty burned homes and stores belonging to the distributors.

News of these protests reached King George and Prime Minister Grenville. They quickly realized that the Stamp Act would be impossible to enforce. Parliament repealed it less than a year after it had been passed into law.

The colonists were wild with delight. The inhabitants of New York City held parades and danced in the streets. Church bells rang out, and the guns of the warships in the harbors boomed joyously from morning till night. Teary-eyed people embraced and congratulated one another. King George went from the role of hated ruler to beloved king. The New York assembly even voted to have a new statue of the king made for the city square.

More Taxes

Although the British had reversed themselves on the Stamp Act, the government was still looking for ways to raise money. In 1766, Parliament passed a new law called the Townshend Act. The act taxed certain goods coming into America from Britain including paper, paint, glass, lead, and tea.

This new tax received no better reception than the first. However, this time the colonists were more confident that they could make Parliament abolish it. The methods that had worked before would be successful again, they were certain.

A boycott began immediately. Instead of buying cloth from British mills, American women spun their own. This homespun, as it was called, was certainly not as colorful or fine as British-made cloth, but it was sturdy and warm.

Tea, a favorite drink of the colonists, was harder to give up. But coffee smuggled in from the Dutch West Indies served as a

The "Other" Adams

It was not surprising that when the delegates to the first Continental Congress were elected, John Adams was at the top of the list. Adams was a well-known Boston lawyer with a highly successful practice. He seemed to have everything—a good career, the respect of his peers, and more than enough money.

His cousin, Samuel Adams, was also elected from the state of Massachusetts. He could not have been more different from his cousin. Although his father had been a wealthy man, Samuel had no head for business. His luck seemed bad, and his money soon ran out. He lived with his wife, Betsy, in a run-down house on Purchase Street in Boston. It was with affection that people called him "the other Adams."

But Adams was a driving force of the Revolution. He was a thinker and a planner. It was he, for instance, who stirred up support for the patriots in Boston after that city was blockaded. "Boston is now suffering in the common cause," he wrote in his letters to leaders in the other colonies. "The liberties of all alike are invaded by the same haughty power!"

The week before Samuel was to go to Philadelphia for the congress, his fellow Bostonians pooled their money and bought him stylish new clothes to replace his worn, rumpled ones. He was given a wig (he had never gotten around to getting one), and his house was painted and fixed up by loving neighbors "in the style a Congressman should live."

Like his better-known cousin, Samuel Adams was also a driving force behind the American Revolution.

substitute. Soon many American families were proudly doing without any British goods at all.

Not all colonists respected the boycott. Many in America remained loyal to the king and were proud of their British ties. These people continued to buy English tea and British linen. But they also ran a risk in doing so—the Sons of Liberty were hard at work watching for enemies of the boycott. Families not participating in the boycott—or even those suspected of not participating—had their houses burned or their windows stoned by members of the Sons of Liberty.

British officials were dismayed at the trouble brewing in the colonies. Things were getting out of hand, and the situation seemed to be growing worse with each passing month. The best solution, they decided, was to send more soldiers to the thirteen colonies to put an end to the rebellion. In late September 1768, a large regiment of British "redcoats" marched off the ship in Boston Harbor. The colonists were concerned. Soldiers had come—not to fight Indians or frighten the French. These soldiers had come to fight *them*.

British redcoats fire on unarmed colonists in the event known as the Boston Massacre.

A "Massacre" in Boston

The British redcoats were not greeted warmly by the colonists. On the contrary, the soldiers were often mocked and taunted on the streets, even by children. Because of their bright scarlet coats, they were often called "Bloodybacks" or "Lobsterbacks." Older children threw rocks or apple cores at the soldiers, who often threw them right back.

On a cold, snowy night on March 5, 1770, the hostility that had been building between redcoats and colonists erupted into violence. A British guard got into a shouting match with a teenage boy on a Boston street. The boy muttered an insult to the soldier, who smacked him with the butt of his musket.

The boy left but returned later with some friends. The shouting and taunting became more and more vicious, and the soldier yelled to his commander to assist him. More colonists gathered, drawn by the shouting, and within a few minutes, what started as a verbal exchange between two people turned into a mob scene. The scene became a near-riot, with the colonists pelting the soldiers with snowballs and rocks.

No historian is quite sure how the shooting started. Perhaps the young British soldiers, nervous and edgy from dealing with the screaming mob, lost their judgment. Or perhaps one of the soldiers heard "Fire!" when the commander yelled "Don't fire!" to his men. But shots did ring out, and within a few seconds, five people in the crowd lay dying in the slushy snow. Six more were severely wounded.

The commanding officer of the redcoats, Capt. Thomas Preston, was charged by the office of the Lieutenant Governor of Boston with murder, as were his troops. In a trial, which some claim was dominated by a pro-British jury, the men were found innocent of all charges.

Fanning the Flames

The British government tried hard after the shooting to bring the situation under control. They repealed the Townshend Act, taking away the tax on everything except tea, to try to appease the angry colonists.

But many of the colonists refused to be appeased. Distinguished members of the Boston community began to talk openly about the British government's injustices. Men like Sons of Liberty organizers Samuel Adams and John Hancock spoke out against "taxation without representation"—the idea that people could be taxed by an assembly in which they were not permitted to send representatives.

Samuel Adams, particularly, was responsible for publicizing the tragic events in Boston. Terming the shootings a "massacre,"

A list of the American dead and wounded in the Boston Massacre.

Adams published pamphlets decrying the soldiers' treatment of the unarmed, "defenseless" Americans. These pamphlets were enthusiastically received by the people of Boston.

Paul Revere, a local silversmith and engraver, was also responsible for stirring up anti-British feelings. Although inaccurate, his drawing of grinning redcoats shooting down peaceful crowds of people was popularly embraced by Bostonians.

All Because of Tea

Supported by the work of Adams and other patriots, the colonists' boycott of tea was working by 1773. More than seventeen million pounds of tea were spoiling in damp warehouses in England. The British government was not making money. How could it on an item that few were buying? The already-crippled British economy was faltering.

By this time there was a new political leader in Britain, Lord Frederick North. After succeeding Grenville as prime minister, Lord North came up with a plan in 1773 that he thought would solve at least part of the problem.

He gave the British East India Company exclusive rights to sell tea to the Americans. (Before, American merchants had bought tea through British business representatives.) By eliminating the middleman, Lord North estimated that the price of tea would go down, even below what smugglers were charging. The tea would still be taxed, but the Americans would not mind, for the price would still be low.

But the Americans were not fooled. "Does he think us that foolish," asked one merchant from Philadelphia, "that we are ignorant to his schemes? He merely wants the smuggler gone, and his hated tax around our necks!"

"Boston Harbor a Teapot Tonight!"

Lord North's solution angered many Americans. In more than one seaport city, crowds chanting "Resist, resist!" refused to let British ships unload the hated tea.

The most famous action against British tea came on December 16, 1773. At a town meeting in Boston, Samuel Adams was addressing the crowd about the tea tax. At one point, Adams said, "This meeting can do nothing more to save the country." This statement was a prearranged signal to the Sons of Liberty. Cries of "Boston Harbor a teapot tonight!" and "Saltwater tea for us all, boys!" rang out. It was time for action.

Later that evening about two hundred men marched toward the docks. So that they would not be recognized, they wore the disguise of Mohawk Indians, their faces darkened by soot and

Lord North (below) tried to cut the price of British tea to make it more palatable to American colonists, but they were not fooled. On December 16, 1773, to rebel against British taxes, colonists dumped dozens of crates of tea into Boston Harbor (bottom).

decorated with war paint. Exactly who the men were has been somewhat of a mystery. Many historians believe they were members of the Sons of Liberty, organized for the event by Samuel Adams and his cohorts.

The group was surprisingly well organized—not boisterous, as one might expect a costumed mob to be. George Hewes, who took part in the event, wrote later that there were three participants "who assumed an authority to direct our operations, to which we readily submitted. They divided us into three parties, for the purpose of boarding the three ships which contained the tea at the same time."

Once on board the three British ships, the men were ordered by their commanders to open the hatches, take out the tea, and throw it overboard.

"We immediately proceeded to execute his orders," said Hewes, "first cutting and splitting the chests with our tomahawks, so as thoroughly to expose them to the effects of the water."

The ships' crews made no move to defend their cargo as the colonists dumped the chests one after another into the harbor. "They had no quarrel with us," said one colonist. "Ours was not a demonstration against those fellows, but against their king and his tax. We were not eager to fall into battle with any...of them."

Men who were there, either as "Mohawks" or as witnesses on the docks, said later that the "Boston Tea Party" was not mean spirited. Leaders of the event swept up the mess on the decks afterwards. In addition, all the men were warned by their commanders that stealing the tea was forbidden. One man, caught by his friends hiding tea leaves in the lining of his jacket, was stripped naked and given a mud bath as a punishment.

The tea party lasted almost three hours. The following day an excited John Adams wrote in his diary: "This is the most magnificent Movement of all. There is a Dignity, a Majesty, a Sublimity in this last Effort of the Patriots that I greatly admire."

"They Ought to Be Knocked About Their Ears"

Britain had given in to the colonists on the Stamp Act and the Townshend Act. But this time the king was in no mood to bargain. Many members of Parliament were also angered by the colonists' rebellion. "It was the most wanton and unprovoked insult offered to the civil power that is recorded in history," snorted one member.

In response to the tea party, the British government passed a series of four Coercive Acts, or "Intolerable" Acts as they were known in the colonies. The acts were aimed at Massachusetts in particular, where the most serious rebellions were taking place.

One of the acts changed the capital of the colony. As a way of demeaning Boston, the British crown announced that the city of Salem would be the new capital. King George and Parliament also ended self-rule in Massachusetts. Any further lawmaking decisions would be made by a king-appointed governor. Another of the Intolerable Acts allowed private buildings in Massachusetts to be used by British soldiers. Private homes, schools, churches—all could be used as barracks without permission of the people.

And the final act, the most despised of all, was the closing of Boston Harbor until all the tea that had been thrown into the harbor was paid for by the people of Boston. Closing the harbor cut the city off from all sea trade and made land access difficult as well.

Boston sailors and fishermen were not allowed to put out to sea. And if they could not do business, then the countless merchants who depended on the fishing and shipping industries would suffer also. These measures effectively assured the destruction of the Boston economy.

Lt. Gen. Thomas Gage and four thousand soldiers were sent to the colonies to enforce the Intolerable Acts.

Such measures were harsh, as Lord North and the king knew. They expected that the troops already in Boston would need help enforcing the Intolerable Acts. Britain sent Lt. Gen. Thomas Gage and four thousand soldiers to Boston. Gage was to command the troops and to act as the new governor of Massachusetts.

Gage had lived in the colonies for eighteen years. He had fought alongside Americans in the French and Indian War. Gage had no doubts that the people of Boston would give in once he and his men arrived. "They are a people who have ever been bold in council," he remarked, "but never remarkable for feats in action."

Gage and his men received a cool reception in Boston. Church bells in Boston tolled the death knell, usually reserved for important funerals in the city. Colonists wore black badges to show they were in mourning.

"I Am Not a Virginian, but an American!"

Since the British targeted only Massachusetts for punishment, it would have been easy for the other colonies to look the other way. Up to this point, the separate colonies had really never been interested in the troubles of the others. The colonies were accustomed to solving their problems individually.

But something unusual happened in 1774. Colonists in New York, Pennsylvania, Rhode Island, and other places debated the events in Boston. They worried that what was occurring in Boston could just as easily occur in their own towns. People in the other colonies began to see an advantage to sticking together. The thirteen quarrelsome, independent colonies began to see the possibility of a single, united nation.

In the little town of Kingston, New Hampshire, people met to draft a letter of support for the people of Boston. "As we look on the late unjust, cruel, hostile and tyrannical acts of the British Parliament," said the letter, "from them clearly we see what the whole continent has to expect under their operation."

In Virginia a young, redheaded colonist named Patrick Henry stood up in the House of Burgesses and said, "The distinctions between Virginians, Pennsylvanians, New Yorkers, New Englanders are no more. I am not a Virginian, but an American!"

More and more people were feeling the same way. Other colonies came to Boston's rescue. They ignored the troops and sent corn, barley, sheep, hogs, and cattle. The supplies came by land to avoid the harbor entirely.

The Continental Congress

Such cooperation must have surprised the British, who thought of the thirteen colonies as "the thirteen quarrelsome sisters," as one member of Parliament called them. The British government reacted by becoming stricter with the rest of the colonies. The Virginia House of Burgesses, for instance, was formally shut down as a punishment for voting to help the people of Boston.

But the colonies could not be so easily controlled. The representatives of Virginia decided to meet on the sly at a tavern in Williamsburg, Virginia. It was there that they proposed the formation of a new group—the Continental Congress. This congress would include representatives from any colony that chose to participate.

Patrick Henry stands before the House of Burgesses in Virginia and declares himself "not a Virginian, but an American!" In this illustration, other Virginians at the assembly receive Henry's declaration with mixed emotions.

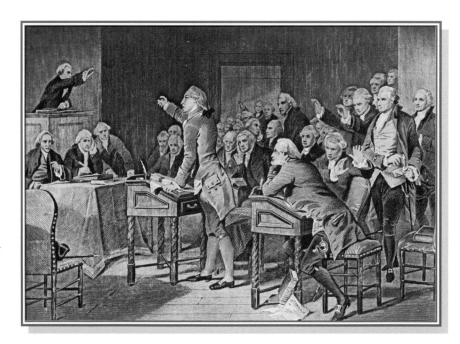

The First Continental Congress meets in Philadelphia. In the early meetings of the congress, members still hoped to make peace with Britain.

"A Congress should be appointed," resolved the Virginia representatives, "from all the Colonies to concert a general and uniform plan for the defense and preservation of our common rights."

The idea met with approval from most of the other colonies. Twelve of the thirteen colonies did want to be part of the Continental Congress. (Only Georgia did not send representatives.) Fifty-four delegates met in Carpenters' Hall in Philadelphia in the fall of 1774. The roster read like a *Who's Who* of American history.

George Washington was a representative from Virginia. Benjamin Franklin came from Pennsylvania. John Adams and his cousin Samuel Adams represented Massachusetts.

The delegates voted to formally denounce the Intolerable Acts. They also decided to step up the boycott of British goods. The purpose of the congress was not to demand independence, however. Members still believed that peace could be achieved. They thought King George and Lord North would become more reasonable and put a stop to their harsh treatment of the colonies.

Moving Toward War

As members of the Continental Congress tried to find peaceful solutions, colonists all over America wondered if the closing of Boston Harbor would lead to a military conflict. In every town and village, militias formed. In the town squares, men drilled, marched, and talked about "how to whip those Lobsterbacks and send them home to George!"

The gradual disharmony between Britain and her colonies was becoming a frenzied, fast-paced march to war. And it did not appear that anything could be done to set it right again.

CHAPTER TWO

America at War

By early 1775, war was like a scent in the air. It was the topic of conversation in every tavern, every shop, and around every dinner table. More and more people who had considered themselves loyal subjects of the king were feeling less British and more American.

"I know not where the sensation began," wrote a clergyman from Philadelphia. "But notions of war that would have made me faint merely twelve months ago now flutter like wings in my breast! I am not afraid, nay, almost exhilarated!"

And while many Americans talked about war, many others were physically preparing for it. Groups of patriots were busy by night stealing muskets and gunpowder from British storehouses. The patriots' job was made easier by many of the redcoats, who were always in need of money. The redcoats would offer to sell their weapons and even their uniforms to any patriot with cash.

The military supplies were stashed in barns throughout the countryside around Boston. No one knew when the war would begin, but everyone wanted to be prepared. In other colonies, patriots began speaking out about getting ready for war, too.

In Richmond, Virginia, Patrick Henry spoke before other assembly members in March 1775. He wanted Virginians to follow the lead of the people of Massachusetts. It was difficult to persuade some of his colleagues, however, for many of them believed that it was more important to preserve peace than to fight for a cause. To these people, Henry said, "Is life so dear, or peace so sweet, as to be purchased at the price of chains

Patrick Henry

Patrick Henry was perhaps the most capable, articulate, and charismatic public speaker during the days of the American Revolution. It was he who coined the phrase, "Give me liberty or give me death," which was met by roars of approval from his fellow patriots.

Like that of other patriot leaders, Henry's background was not impressive. He was born on the Virginia frontier and educated at home by his mother. As a young man, he tried a few different occupations—including operating a store and farming—but was not good at any of them. What he really enjoyed was talking with people—arguing about ideas and opinions.

So great was his love of discussion, in fact, that it contributed to his failure as a store clerk. One day, while stretched out full length on a large sack of salt, Henry was enjoying himself, deep in a debate with his friends. A customer came in and asked Henry if he had any salt in the store. According to the story, Henry broke off talking just long enough to shake his head, "No," he said, "just sold the last pack."

At the age of twenty-three, Henry acquired an old law book. He read it between the hours he helped at his father-in-law's tavern. After studying it for six weeks, he decided that he would be a lawyer. He traveled to Williamsburg to ask the legal examiners there to give him a license.

The four legal examiners did not use written tests to measure a candidate's ability. Instead, each examiner took a turn interviewing the candidate. To be granted a license, at least two of the examiners had to agree to sign it.

Two of the examiners ended the interviews with Henry very quickly. They saw, in the opening minutes, that Henry had not studied law—that he knew only what was in the one law book. And even his knowledge of that book was scant. In addition, Henry's appearance made him look careless. His hair was too long, and his clothing, cheap. He was tall and gawky and grinned at the examiners—quite a difference from the somber, studious candidates whom the examiners usually saw.

But Henry impressed the other two. He entered into a debate on an interpretation of law with examiner John Randolph. Henry merely stated what appeared to him to be common sense. Randolph disagreed, and they consulted one of the large law books in Randolph's office.

Patrick Henry loved political discussion and debate. Here, he delivers his great speech before the Virginia assembly, concluding with the words, "Give me liberty or give me death."

After paging through it, Randolph looked up at Henry with respect. "You have never seen these books," Randolph told him, "nor this principle of law. Yet you are right and I am wrong. And from this lesson you have given me—you must excuse me for saying it—I will never trust to appearance again."

The license was granted, and Henry began what became a highly successful law career. In his first three years, he tried 1,185 cases and won most of them. Within two years, the gawky redhead was the most sought-after lawyer in Virginia.

and slavery? Forbid it, Almighty God! I know not what course others may take; but as for me, give me liberty or give me death!" Henry's words stirred the Virginia assembly, which voted to prepare to fight.

The First Strike

British commander Gage had learned from spies that the patriots had been hoarding guns and ammunition in two small villages northwest of Boston—Lexington and Concord. He meant to confiscate the weapons before they could be used against his troops.

Secrecy was extremely important to Gage's mission. No one except the highest-level British soldiers knew when the British would march to confiscate the weapons. If the partriots had warning, Gage knew, they would have time to move the supplies.

But secrecy was almost impossible in a city like Boston. All eyes were on the British. The patriots had spies throughout the town. Shopkeepers, street vendors, and others listened to every word the British soldiers said. Every conversation, every casual comment, any unusual preparations would quickly be reported.

By April 17, various bits of information from a variety of sources indicated that the British might soon be striking the villages of Lexington and Concord. Spies had overheard officers talking about "teaching the rebels a lesson they'll need to remember." Taken together, all the scraps of information led patriot leaders to anticipate a British invasion by water. From Boston, the British would head east to Cambridge, then by land to Lexington and Concord.

Messages were hastily relayed to Lexington and Concord, and weapons were relocated. Some were hidden in cellars and under hay stacks; some were even buried under plowed fields.

Sure enough, patriots in Boston witnessed boatloads of British troops leaving Boston Harbor. They quickly told leaders of the Sons of Liberty, who sent messengers on horseback to Lexington and Concord to alert citizens there. Paul Revere is the most famous of these horsemen, but there were two others. A shoemaker named William Dawes and Dr. Samuel Prescott also made the midnight journey yelling, "The regulars are out!"

Although he is credited with making the entire journey through the countryside, Paul Revere was not the most successful of the three riders. Revere met up with Dawes and Prescott after warning the citizens of Lexington. Half a mile out of town, the three rode straight into a group of British scouts.

Dawes escaped, riding safely back to Lexington. Prescott jumped over a stone fence and evaded the British. He was able to reach Concord to warn the citizens there. But Revere was captured. The British scouts did not harm him, letting him go after

Paul Revere makes his famous ride. Although he is the rider most people are familiar with, Revere was not the most successful. William Dawes and Samuel Prescott were the two riders who completed their missions, while Revere was captured by British scouts.

an hour. They did, however, have the wisdom to cut the girth strap of his saddle so he would be unable to ride any farther.

"Lay Down Your Weapons, You Damned Rebels!"

After being alerted to the soldiers' approach, the villagers of Lexington and Concord made no secret of the fact that they knew the British troops were on their way. Signal guns boomed, and church bells tolled noisily. British Maj. John Pitcairn, having hoped for a surprise attack, was furious.

Marching into Lexington, the British were met by about seventy armed patriots. Major Pitcairn shouted to the Americans to drop their weapons. A few did, but most stood firm.

"Lay down your arms, you damned rebels, and disperse!" Pitcairn reportedly yelled. The Americans continued to stand their ground. Both sides exchanged curses and angry taunts.

No one is certain who fired the first shot, but it has been called "the shot heard 'round the world." It was the beginning of a battle that lasted less than five minutes. When the shooting was over,

The British expected little resistance when they marched to Lexington and Concord, but the Americans were forewarned and prepared to attack. At the Battle of Lexington (right), about seventy colonists opposed the British soldiers. At Concord (top), Americans again fought the British.

eight colonists were dead. One British soldier had been slightly wounded, and Major Pitcairn's horse had been grazed by a bullet.

The British marched quickly from Lexington to Concord. They found very little of the patriots' cache of weapons—a few muskets were the extent of it. These they burned and then they prepared to march back to Boston.

As they began their march, more than one hundred Sons of Liberty were quietly waiting. They watched as the straight, even lines of British troops approached them.

One member named Thaddeus Blood later recalled, "We saw the British a-coming. The sun was rising and shined on their arms, and they made a noble appearance in their red coats and glistening arms."

As the British got closer to the militia, the Americans began firing. The Americans clearly had the advantage, for they were fighting as they had learned to fight from the Indians—without letting the enemy see them. They hid behind trees and rocks, in bushes, and under bridges.

The British were confused by the onslaught. It was not the fighting style they were accustomed to. In Europe, soldiers fought from straight, even lines, one behind the other. As soldiers fell in the front, soldiers stepped forward to take their places. It was very orderly. This day, the British fought the way they had been trained, but it was not effective.

To the British soldiers, the Americans seemed like phantoms. One British soldier later wrote home complaining that the Americans did not know how "to wage a fair and honest fight." Another said that it was "as if men came down from the clouds." The heavy fog of gunpowder in the air was like a blanket muffling the sound of muskets and the shouts of the soldiers. All along the sixteen-mile route back to Boston, the British were shot at by the elusive patriots. The march suddenly became a quick retreat, with redcoats falling at every turn.

The British finally reached their destination and the protecting guns of their warships in the harbor. Their losses had been staggering—99 dead or missing and 174 wounded. The Americans' losses were lighter, with 52 dead and 41 wounded.

The patriots' attack at Concord startled the British. They had expected to surprise the patriots and, as one British soldier wrote, "give the Rebels a good high Drubbing for the trouble they cause." The British had underestimated the Americans. Newspapers in London had called the patriots "feeble."

The Battle of Lexington lasted less than five minutes. When it was over, eight colonists were dead.

Knowing this, Benjamin Franklin remarked, "His [General Gage's] troops made a most vigorous retreat—twenty miles in three hours—scarce to be paralleled in history. The feeble Americans, who pelted them all the way, could scarcely keep up with them."

Boston colonists were jubilant over the outcome of the battles at Lexington and Concord. Church bells rang, and fireworks were set off. The war had begun, and the patriots had done well. Men from other New England colonies were arriving at the American camp near Boston. They, too, wanted to fight the British.

Yet even as patriots were enlisting to fight, many others were hoping further bloodshed could be avoided. In May, 1775, a month after the battle at Lexington and Concord, the Continental Congress drafted an urgent message to King George. (Urgent messages took as long to get to England as nonurgent ones— about eight weeks by ship.) They begged the king to stop future aggressions against the colonies. Unfortunately, the king's eventual answer was curt. He sent back a reply formally breaking ties with the colonies, calling the patriots "wicked and desperate persons." There seemed no alternative but to stage an armed revolt against the British.

The British beat a hasty retreat as patriots shoot at them from all directions during the Battle of Concord (below). A list of dead and wounded from the battle (left) is printed on a broadside.

A LIST of the Names of the PROVINCIALS who were Killed and Wounded in the late Engagement with His Majesty's Troops at Concord, &c.

KILLED.

Of *Lexington.*
* Mr. Robert Munroe,
* Mr. Jonas Parker,
* Mr. Samuel Hadley,
* Mr. Jonas Harrington,
* Mr. Caleb Harrington,
* Mr. Isaac Muzzy,
* Mr. John Brown,
Mr. John Raymond,
Mr. Nathaniel Wyman,
Mr. Jedediah Munroe.

Of *Menotomy.*
Mr. Jason Russel,
Mr. Jabez Wyman,
Mr. Jason Winship.

Of *Sudbury.*
Deacon Haynes,
Mr. —— Reed.

Of *Concord.*
Capt. James Miles.

Of *Bedford.*
Capt. Jonathan Willson.

Of *Acton.*
Capt. Davis,
Mr. —— Hosmer,
Mr. James Howard.

Of *Woburn.*
* Mr. Azael Porter,
Mr. Daniel Thompson.

Of *Charlestown.*
Mr. James Miller,
Capt. William Barber's Son.

Of *Brookline*
Isaac Gardner, Esq;

Of *Cambridge.*
Mr. John Hicks,
Mr. Moses Richardson,
Mr. William Massey.

Of *Medford.*
Mr. Henry Putnam.

Of *Lynn.*
Mr. Abednego Ramsdell,
Mr. Daniel Townsend,
Mr. William Flint,
Mr. Thomas Hadley.

Of *Danvers.*
Mr. Henry Jacobs,
Mr. Samuel Cook,
Mr. Ebenezer Goldthwait,
Mr. George Southwick,
Mr. Benjamin Daland, jun.
Mr. Jotham Webb,
Mr. Perley Putnam.

Of *Salem.*
Mr. Benjamin Peirce.

WOUNDED.

Of *Lexington.*
Mr. John Robbins,
Mr. John Tidd,
Mr. Solomon Peirce,
Mr. Thomas Winship,
Mr. Nathaniel Farmer,
Mr. Joseph Comee,
Mr. Ebenezer Munroe,
Mr. Francis Brown,
Prince Easterbrooks,
(A Negro Man.

Of *Framingham.*
Mr. —— Hemenway.

Of *Bedford.*
Mr. John Lane.

Of *Woburn.*
Mr. George Reed,
Mr. Jacob Bacon.

Of *Medford.*
Mr. William Polly

Of *Lynn.*
Joshua Feit,
Mr. Timothy Munroe.

Of *Danvers.*
Mr. Nathan Putnam,
Mr. Dennis Wallis.

Of *Beverly.*
Mr. Nathaniel Cleaves.

MISSING.

Of *Menotomy.*
Mr. Samuel Frost,
Mr. Seth Russell.

Those distinguished with this Mark [*] were killed by the first fire of the Regulars

Sold in Queen Street.

To Breed's Hill

Because the British occupied Boston, the patriots wanted to take possession of the land surrounding the city. That way, they could keep a lookout on British troop activity and launch their own attacks.

The patriots' army, about eighteen hundred men led by Col. William Prescott, planned to seize nearby Bunker Hill. From atop this hill, they could shoot their heavy cannons across the bay at the city of Boston. After several days of heavy bombardment, the patriots hoped, the British would leave.

The plan might have had a chance, but it was changed at the last moment. An older officer named Israel Putnam offered what he felt was good, sound advice. Putnam felt that it would be foolish to establish themselves on Bunker Hill, for Boston Harbor was too far away for the patriots' cannons to reach. Instead, Putnam advised Prescott's army to fortify a lower hill called Breed's Hill, which was closer to the harbor.

The patriots moved to the area late on June 16. They worked all through the night digging an earthen fortification called a redoubt. At daylight the next day, the British were amazed to see a fort that was not there before.

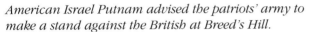

American Israel Putnam advised the patriots' army to make a stand against the British at Breed's Hill.

Immediately the guns on the British warships in the harbor began firing huge, twenty-four-pound cannonballs at Breed's Hill. The British troops, two thousand of them, gathered at the base of the hill and began to march toward the Americans.

The Americans had been instructed to wait until the very last moment to fire their muskets. "Don't fire until you see the whites of their eyes," was the order from Putnam. The patriots waited until the British were less than twenty-five yards from them and opened fire.

The battle of Breed's Hill, mistakenly called the battle of Bunker Hill, was the bloodiest, most violent battle of the entire war. As the precise rows of redcoats attacked, moving in rhythm with their drummer's beat, the patriots shot. One witness remembered afterward that the muskets of the Americans created "a mighty sheet of flames."

Row after row of British soldiers moved up the hill, only to be mowed down by patriot musket fire. American soldiers who were there told later how the grass was slippery with blood.

The patriots feverishly worked throughout the night to fortify Breed's Hill for a stand against the British (right). As the British scale Breed's Hill (below) patriots fire at their orderly rows.

"The Redcoats couldn't keep their footing for the blood did make the grass like sheer ice," wrote one young man from Massachusetts.

Another told how he had trouble hearing anything except the screams. "I listened for the crack of my musket, or the gun of the boy next to me," he wrote. "But all I could hear were the cries, the screams of wounded men. It was louder than the guns, louder even than the cannon."

Twice the British mounted an attack on the hill, and twice they were turned back. The third time, the Americans ran out of ammunition. They fought anyway. Some used the butts of their muskets, others rocks, or fists, or even teeth.

From their position above Breed's Hill, the Americans were able to mow down the advancing British troops (bottom), until they ran out of ammunition. In the hand-to-hand combat that followed (below and right), the British were able to defeat the Americans and take the hill, but at a high cost.

After the initial battles of the Revolution, men of all ages left their farms and families to join in the fight.

In the end, the British gained control of the hill, but at a huge cost. More than one thousand redcoats had been killed or wounded compared with four hundred Americans. What they had to show for it was a hill that was virtually useless.

The Lesson of Breed's Hill

Sir William Howe, the commander of British troops at Breed's Hill, was horrified. He had never seen so much bloodshed. Certainly he had never expected such a devastating loss to his own forces. The experience at Breed's Hill made Howe more tentative and less willing to take risks in future battles. He could never bear the thought of another "victory" like the one at Breed's Hill.

The reaction in Britain was also one of shock. News of the tremendous losses appalled members of Parliament, who had been certain that the British troops would have no trouble with the Americans. One member of Parliament told the prime minister, "Eight more such 'victories' and we shall have no one left to report them!"

It was true. No one in England had expected much of a fight out of the ragtag group of Americans. An assortment of millers, carpenters, and farmers had stood up to thousands of well-trained, professional soldiers. Although the Americans had lost the battle, they had inflicted heavy losses on an enemy that was thought to be in complete control.

Benjamin Franklin

Benjamin Franklin was a politician, a scientist, and an inventor. He spent many years, too, as a diplomat in England and France. Early in the war, Franklin went to France to try to persuade the French government to aid the patriots' cause. He reminded French leaders that if Britain were to win its war with the colonies, it would become stronger than ever before—bad news for the French, who had been enemies of the British for more than a century.

Franklin was persuasive. France began sending military supplies and money to the patriots. This was done secretly through Franklin and his spies, for France did not want to risk backing the Americans if they lost.

Franklin became a much-loved figure in France during his stay there. Whenever he went out, he was trailed by hundreds of admirers, who bargained with one another for the best places to stand along the roadside to see him. Historians say that some French people paid the equivalent of fifty dollars just to catch a glimpse of the stout, balding American.

Franklin's scientific accomplishments are also well known. He proved that lightning was actually electricity. He invented bifocal lenses and came up with the fuel-saving, efficient Franklin stove.

Because of Franklin's many talents, it is not surprising that he was sometimes credited with being more of a genius than he really was. For instance, early in the war, the British heard rumors that Franklin had invented a large electrical machine that was connected to a chain. The chain reportedly stretched between France and England. When Franklin threw the switch, the chain would electrocute the entire British nation.

Another rumor that had many British officials worried was about huge mirrors on the shore of France. The story was that Franklin had set them up to reflect the burning rays of the sun. When he focused the mirrors just right across the English Channel, Franklin would be able to set fire to every British ship in the harbor.

Of course, these stories were nonsense. But as it turned out, Franklin himself had been behind them. He knew British Loyalists were snooping on his desk. Rather than fight the spies, he merely planted such false stories to distract and worry the British.

Perhaps one of the most versatile men of all time, Benjamin Franklin was a diplomat, inventor, scientist, and politician. He was also a popular writer and many of his witty sayings remain in use today.

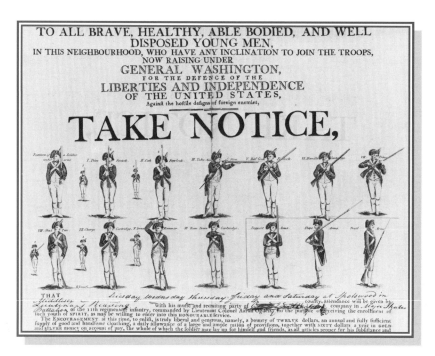

A recruiting notice asks all able-bodied men to enlist in the Continental army. Men of all ages responded to these notices in a fever pitch of patriotism.

Raising the Continental Army

At the same time the battle of Breed's Hill was being fought, the Continental Congress was meeting. Since King George had broken off relations between Britain and the colonies, members of the congress were resigned to the fact that the fighting would continue. The delegates voted to establish a Continental army—one that would be made up of soldiers from all colonies. The battles at Lexington, Concord, and Breed's Hill were evidence that more than just a local militia was needed.

Local volunteer groups in villages and cities throughout the colonies began signing up soldiers to join with Boston's Sons of Liberty against the British. As one Pennsylvania resident wrote in her journal, "There was a fever pitch of patriotism; no one took account of personal risk or unpleasantness."

There were, in many villages, more volunteers than there were muskets. In Virginia there was a sharpshooting contest held to determine who would be permitted to join the army. A Connecticut woman gladly sent five of her sons to fight, saying that she preferred "they all be killed than one come back a coward."

There were no age limits for Americans who wanted to enlist. Pennsylvania's Fourth Company was known as "the Old Man's Regiment." No one in the company was under forty. The regiment's drummer was eighty-four, and the commanding officer was ninety-six.

The Gentleman from Virginia

As important as the soldiers in the army, however, was the choice of a commander to lead them. The Continental Congress made the decision, and it was no easy task. Many considerations had to be weighed.

Certainly the job required a man with military experience. Leadership and courage were important as well. Politics had to be considered, too. The southern colonies were still reluctant to enter into a dispute with Britain. By choosing a commander from the South, the Continental Congress believed it might kindle support there.

At a meeting of the Continental Congress on June 14, 1775, John Adams announced his choice for a commander. He nominated "the gentleman from Virginia"—George Washington.

Witnesses that day said that there were interesting reactions to Adams's choice. Most of them were favorable. Washington, with his quiet, calm way, had impressed many of the congressmen.

There was at least one very disappointed person in the room, however. According to one delegate, Bostonian John Hancock "flushed with mortification and resentment" when Adams nominated Washington. Hancock had hoped to be nominated himself, although he had very little military experience.

Although he did not have much military experience, George Washington was a popular choice to command the Continental army. (Below and bottom) Washington greets American troops upon taking command.

The Quiet Giant

Most people envision George Washington as he appears on the one-dollar bill. Actually, that picture is from a portrait painted when he was much older than he was during his years as a general.

Washington was not handsome, but he was striking. At six feet two inches tall, weighing over two hundred pounds, he was considered remarkably large for an eighteenth-century man. (The average height for a man in 1776 was five feet five inches.)

His hair was reddish blond, although he usually wore a white wig, as did most men of the day. He had fair skin with ruddy patches across his nose caused by scars from smallpox, a disease he had had as a boy.

Although Washington did not have a great deal of military experience, he was a good leader. He had a reputation of being an extremely fair man willing to listen to all sides of an issue. A good friend of Washington, Thomas Jefferson, once described him as "a wise, a good, and a great man."

He cared a great deal about the welfare of his soldiers, and they knew it. "Few of us like the man, but we all love him," wrote one soldier in a letter. "The General walks by and we all feel honored. I have the feeling he would risk his life for any man, even the lowliest among us."

It was Washington who wrote letters by the hundreds to congress reminding them over and over to send supplies to his raggedy men. "These soldiers eat every kind of horse food but hay," he wrote angrily. "The fortitude—the long and great suffering of this army—is unexampled in history."

And on the battlefield, Washington was a master. He seemed to know when to fight and when it was best to slip away and save his men to fight another day. He knew, too, when his men were losing heart in a battle they needed to win and was quick to encourage them. "Good, brave fellows!" he would shout, as he urged them on.

His leadership was acknowledged by more people than just his soldiers. Frederick the Great, the most renowned military leader of Prussia, was amazed at Washington's ability to turn strategic retreats into victories. He sent Washington an ornate sword with the inscription: "From the oldest General in the world to the best."

For all of his leadership abilities, it seems surprising that Washington was as quiet as he was. He spoke only when he had something of importance to say; he was not comfortable with easy chatter.

Historians say that his reluctance to speak publicly was because of his teeth. Since his twenties, Washington had been plagued by bad teeth, and most of them had to be pulled. He did have false teeth, but they never fit properly.

Throughout his adult life, his dentists tried all kinds of materials, from wood or ivory to animal teeth like elk and pig. Washington even had a pair set in lead, which weighed three pounds and was connected with springs made of steel. Nothing worked, however, so he spent his life in discomfort.

George Washington will always be remembered as one of the most important individuals in the founding of the United States. George Washington was a rare individual—a person who was a great thinker as well as a man of action on the battlefield.

Washington reacted with characteristic shyness. According to historian Donald Sobol, as soon as Adams nominated him, Washington "dashed in to the library adjoining the chamber from his usual modesty."

Washington's military experience was not vast. He had served in the French and Indian War twenty years before. He had not commanded large groups of men as he would with the Continental army. Instead, his command had been limited to twenty or thirty men at a time.

Nonetheless, Washington was a popular choice, and he was unanimously elected by the congress. In his acceptance speech the following day, Washington told the congress that he was concerned that his experience and ability were not equal to the task.

"However," Washington said, "as the Congess desires I will enter upon the momentous duty, and exert every power I Possess In their Service for the Support of the glorious Cause…. I beg it be remembered by every Gentleman in the room, that I this declare with the utmost sincerity, I do not think myself equal to the Command I am honoured with."

He also refused any pay. He told the congress that he did not wish to make any profit. "I will keep an exact Account of my expences," he promised, "those I doubt not they will [pay back] and that is all I desire."

Driving the British from Boston

Washington's first task was to get his army into fighting shape. A good army needs discipline, and the Continental army needed it even more. So many of the men were independent farmers that they were not used to taking orders from anyone. In addition, because the men had come from all over the country, they were at first uncomfortable together and lacked confidence in one another.

Over the next months, Washington worked hard to build camps and organize weapons and other materials for war. He also began drilling and training his soldiers. Washington knew that beating the British would be the hardest thing these men would ever do.

Early in 1776, Washington was eager to get into battle. The situation had remained in a deadlock. The British were in control of Boston but had not ventured away from the city since the battle of Breed's Hill. Washington wanted to force the British out. But without heavy artillery, the patriots could not hope to make a move against the entrenched redcoats. Washington thought he knew where he could get the artillery, however.

Seven months before, a group of patriots calling themselves the Green Mountain Boys, under the command of a young man named Ethan Allen, had taken over Fort Ticonderoga, an old fort

The capture of Fort Ticonderoga in New York (top) was easy—only a few British soldiers lived there. But getting the seized artillery pieces to Boston where they were needed was an amazing feat led by Col. Henry Knox (above).

in upstate New York. Fort Ticonderoga had been important in the French and Indian War, but in 1775 was in disrepair. Only a skeleton crew of British soldiers lived there, and they were not prepared for the attack.

Seizing the fort had been easy. Only a British sentry was hurt; otherwise the event was bloodless. "My first thought was to kill him with my sword," said Allen later, "but, in an instant, I altered the design and fury of the blow to a slight cut on the side of the head, upon which he dropped his gun."

The British were rounded up as prisoners, and the Continental Congress sent one thousand soldiers to hold the fort. At the fort were storehouses of large artillery pieces, and now, in January 1776, Washington knew they were just what he needed.

Washington sent one of his best officers, Col. Henry Knox, to bring the cannons and other artillery back to Boston. The task was exceptionally difficult. It involved hauling heavy equipment over three hundred miles of ice-covered wilderness. Knox knew Washington and the rest of the army depended on him to deliver the weapons.

Barges and sleds were used to travel across the waterways of New York and the snowy hills of New England in the dead of winter. As historian Robert Leckie writes, "When the barges sank,

Using barges and sleds, Colonel Knox and his men managed to haul cannons and other artillery over three hundred miles from Fort Ticonderoga in New York to General Washington's troops in Boston.

the guns were dredged up; when the sleds broke through the ice, they were fished up once more; and when oxen died in the traces or men broke their bones manhandling the cannon up and down snow-covered slopes, replacements were found to take their place."

The cannons and other guns were set up on hills above Boston. On the night of March 2, 1776, American forces began bombarding Boston. The British were stunned. They had had no idea what the Americans had been up to, and they were unsure of what their response should be.

Finally, General Howe made the decision to evacuate Boston. The British got on board 175 ships in Boston Harbor and sailed north to Halifax, Nova Scotia. Many of the patriots cheered, for they were sure they had beaten the redcoats.

George Washington knew better.

Back, with Reinforcements

Washington was certain that the British would be back. The British had had to leave because there was no way they could have held Boston. But by leaving they had time to plan a new strategy and get reinforcements.

The new target, Washington felt, would be New York City. It was the best seaport in the colonies and was a key center of trade. Too, whoever controlled New York controlled the Hudson River.

Thomas Jefferson

Except for Benjamin Franklin, no man in American history has contributed such a wide variety of services to his country as Thomas Jefferson has.

Jefferson was a politician and a statesman. He was one of the most talented architects of his time, designing the Virginia state capitol, the University of Virginia, and his own home, Monticello. He loved music and was an accomplished violinist. He invented a type of plow, a lap desk, and a device for decoding secret messages. He was also interested in languages and compiled several vocabulary lists of Native American languages. Jefferson's most well-known contribution to the United States, however, was as the author of the Declaration of Independence.

In the summer of 1776, the Continental Congress appointed a committee to draw up a formal declaration of independence to be sent to King George. Jefferson was one of five men appointed. When the time came for one man to actually write the declaration, Jefferson told John Adams that he, Adams, should do it.

"I will not," Adams said.

"You should do it," Jefferson said.

"Oh, no!" Adams shook his head.

"Why will you not?" Jefferson persisted. "You ought to do it."

"I will not."

"Why?" asked Jefferson.

"Reasons enough," Adams replied.

Jefferson looked at Adams carefully. "What can be your reasons?"

John Adams listed them for Jefferson: "Reason first, you are a Virginian, and a Virginian ought to appear at the head of this business. Reason second, I am obnoxious, suspected and unpopular. You are very much otherwise. Reason third, you can write ten times better than I can."

Jefferson spoke up at once. "Well, if you are decided, I will do as well as I can."

Jefferson wrote the Declaration in the second-story room he had rented on Market Street in Philadelphia. He wrote in a neat, though rather small, penmanship. When the draft was done, he showed his fellow committee members. They made minor changes, and Jefferson did not have to revise very much of it. It was approved by the congress as "a fine piece of work, well done."

One of the revisions Jefferson had to make was a section in which he condemned slavery as immoral. Jefferson believed the practice of slavery was wrong. He never freed his own slaves, though, for he did not feel that blacks should be completely free to mingle with whites.

Thomas Jefferson can truly be said to have been the voice of the Revolution. A skilled and eloquent writer, the author of the Declaration of Independence penned many other memorable pieces in defense of America's independence.

British ships could carry redcoats north on the Hudson, and they could mount an attack on New England colonies from the west.

Washington sent a large portion of his army to New York to wait for the British to return. By June and July, ships carrying thousands of British sailors and soldiers—forty-five thousand in all—sailed into New York's harbor exactly where Washington had anticipated.

At least twelve thousand of the soldiers on board the ships were from Germany. (The British were having difficulty recruiting enough soldiers from Britain, so they were forced to "import" some.) In those days, Germany was not a single nation but rather a group of states, each with its own government. Many of the states were poor and sold the war services of their young men to make money. In return for these services, each German ruler would get a set fee. If the soldier died in battle, the ruler would make about $22.75—a nice profit for the government.

These soldiers were dressed in odd metal helmets, and they all had long braided ponytails hanging down to their waists. The colonists called them Hessians after the place in Germany from which they came.

The Hessians did not speak much English and were treated poorly by the British. To make them fight harder, British officers told them horror stories about the Americans. Many Hessians believed, for instance, that the Americans ate their prisoners. To avoid this fate, Hessians quickly shot every American taken prisoner.

Formally Independent

While the American army spent the hot summer months of 1776 waiting and watching the arrival of the British, the Continental Congress was busy voting to declare Americans free of British rule. Although many colonists still had hopes that a settlement with the king could be worked out, many former loyal subjects were ready for independence.

"How can we playact and pretend any longer," wrote one New York woman, "thinking our brothers in England are willing to listen to us? Freedom is in the hearts of the children and on the lips of us all."

The Continental Congress voted to send a formal declaration to King George outlining the reasons for their dissatisfaction. Members of the congress asked a young thirty-three-year-old from Virginia, Thomas Jefferson, to write the declaration.

In his autobiography, John Adams recalled that Jefferson was not a good speaker: "The most of a Speech he ever made in my hearing was a gross insult on Religion…for which I gave him immediately the Reprehension which he richly merited." However, Jefferson was a gifted writer, who "had the Reputation of a masterly Pen."

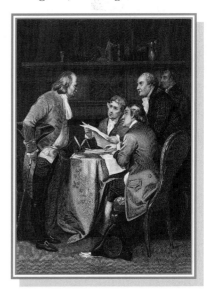

The five-man drafting committee works on the Declaration of Independence. From left to right are Benjamin Franklin, Thomas Jefferson, John Adams, Robert Livingston, and Roger Sherman.

(Top) The Declaration of Independence is signed on July 4, 1776. (Bottom) The document is read to Washington's Continental army on July 9.

The Declaration of Independence went through some revisions and was signed on July 4, 1776. The members of the Continental Congress knew that what they were doing was dangerous; in fact, it was considered treason, a crime of the utmost seriousness.

The punishment for treason against the British was astonishing. Criminals were hanged until they were almost dead. Soldiers then cut them down and cut out their intestines, setting them on fire before their eyes. They were beheaded and cut into four pieces. Each piece was then put on a spike and displayed for all to witness.

There must have been a great deal of tension in the room where the Declaration of Independence was signed. Heavyset Benjamin Harrison, a delegate from Virginia, declared that his weight for once gave him an advantage over the thinner signers. He laughingly told skinny Congressman Elbridge Gerry from Massachusetts that he would die more quickly because he was fat. "All will be over with me in a moment," said Harrison, "but you will be kicking in the air half an hour after I am gone!"

The formal announcement to King George was a dangerous and difficult step. But the years ahead would be more difficult. Simply declaring independence was not enough. The colonists had to fight for true freedom from the British crown.

CHAPTER THREE

The Price of Independence

The Declaration of Independence stated that the thirteen colonies wished to be free of British rule. Not all of the colonists were eager to break ties with Britain, however. In 1776, only about one-third of Americans were willing to go to war with the British. Another third were fence straddlers. They were unsure of how they felt and waited to see how the war would go before committing themselves.

Americans vs. Americans

The remaining third considered themselves loyal to King George and were known as Loyalists. Loyalists were proud to be British subjects, although they were often critical of how Britain treated the colonies. Like the patriots, Loyalists protested against the Stamp Act, the coming of the redcoats, and other British acts against America. But they did not want to become independent or to fight to get that way.

The Loyalists were not treated well in the colonies, especially once war broke out. Patriots usually referred to Loyalists as "Tories," an Irish word for a bandit or thief. In the words of one eighteenth-century comic, a Tory was "a thing whose head is in England, whose body is in America, and whose neck needs stretching!"

Many Tories were reluctant to make their views public, for mobs of patriots could be dangerous. Stories abound of Tories who were whipped and beaten by groups of colonists. Their homes were sometimes burned, their businesses ransacked or destroyed, and their children threatened.

Many Tories were spies for the British; many others were willing to join the redcoats in fighting their patriot neighbors and friends. Some moved back to England or up into Canada. They often found it too difficult to remain in the colonies where they were identified as traitors—enemies of the Revolution.

The concern over whether one's neighbor may be a Tory spy was troublesome in the colonies. Often there was a witch-hunt atmosphere in which people would start rumors about strangers or people they did not like.

Joseph Penn, a shopkeeper from New York, wrote in 1776 that "I have heard the word 'Tory' pass from ear to ear, and I know not whether it can be believed. Is it a debtor who is the victim of the vile rumor? An unscrupulous merchant? Or is the rumor true, and the poor soul is rightly accused?"

One Loyalist complained, "I have had the misfortune to affront one of the Committee men, by not giving his Daughter a kiss.... This has offended the old man so much, that...he has several spies to watch my actions. Sorry I did not give the ugly Jade a kiss."

A large statue of King George is pulled off its pedestal by enthusiastic patriots. The statue was later melted down and used for bullets for the Continental army.

Fighting in New York

Once news of the Declaration spread, patriots enthusiastically prepared for war. A large statue of King George was pulled down with ropes, and its metal was melted down for bullets for the Continental army. "We shall give them a chance to feel melted Majesty fired at them!" crowed one patriot.

However, the enthusiasm did not last long. By August 22, the British had landed a sizable force on Long Island, New York. Even though the Americans had been expecting to battle the British at New York, the first real encounter was a disaster for the Continental army.

The Americans had set up two lines across the western side of Long Island. The strongest line overlooked the East River and was well within cannon range of Manhattan. This should have put the Americans in a strong position, if not for a mistake in planning.

When the attack came at dawn on August 27, this mistake became evident. There was only a handful of soldiers posted on the left flank of the line. British soldiers had no trouble killing them and pouring through the American line. They attacked the Americans from both the front and back. One soldier from Maryland wrote later, "The British then advanced within 300 yards of

The Battle of Long Island was a devastating loss for the Americans. Through an error of bad planning, the Continental army was caught in British crossfire between the front and the back.

After the Battle of Long Island, Washington got a regiment of fishermen to row his troops across the East River to Manhattan Island during the night.

us and began a very heavy fire from their cannon and mortars; for both the balls and shells flew very fast, now and then taking off a head."

The frantic American troops were caught in a cross fire and were falling in lifeless heaps. General Washington, watching from a hill nearby, reportedly wrung his hands and cried, "Good God! What Brave fellows I must this day lose!"

General Howe could easily have finished off the American army at Long Island. Eyewitnesses to the battle remembered later that British soldiers were begging Howe to let them fight on. But Howe, remembering the slaughter at Breed's Hill, would not allow it.

Howe was certain that he was in a position to demand the Americans' surrender the next day. He ordered his men to dig trenches and wait rather than continue the assault. Howe was confident that the Americans were beaten and would soon admit it.

However, in the heavy fog that August night, Washington and his men pulled a disappearing act. He ordered a regiment made up of fishermen from Massachusetts to row the army across the East River to Manhattan Island.

While Howe and his men dug in, waiting for a white flag of surrender, Washington's forces—all ninety-five hundred of them—slipped away into the mist. Although he had certainly lost the battle, Washington had saved his remaining troops to fight another day. Washington had also earned a reputation as "a sly old fox"—a fact that embarrassed and angered the British.

Losing Faith

Over the following weeks, the British pushed the American troops farther and farther back. Forts that Washington had thought were secure dropped easily into British control. Skirmishes were fought, and each time the Americans lost. The Continental army was shoved back into New Jersey and finally across the Delaware River into Pennsylvania.

By late November, Washington's losses were staggering. In three months his army had lost thousands of men, and a total of five thousand were taken prisoner. Although he always managed to slip away before his army was entirely defeated, Washington knew that he could not go on much longer.

The morale of the patriots was at an all-time low. They had been confident and aggressive at Breed's Hill but were now ragged and demoralized after further battles with the British. One soldier from Connecticut wrote in his journal in 1776,

The landing of British forces in the Jerseys on November 20, 1776. New Jersey became British-held territory after the Continental army suffered a series of defeats.

"I know we must go on, but many have given up. Yesterday we saw a neighbor beheaded by a 24-pound cannonball. Those redcoats kill us so easily."

A Desperation Move

Washington knew that to maintain the morale of his troops, he would have to pull off a victory. Late in December 1776, Washington decided to use what few men he still had to surprise the British. Howe had his men in winter quarters. Little fighting was done in winter, and armies would go into winter quarters and wait until spring to resume the war.

The American soldiers were exhausted and starving. Many had no warm clothes and were suffering from exposure to the cold. Howe was confident that Washington's army would not survive the winter, much less pose a threat to him in the spring.

Washington hoped that by attacking the redcoats when they least expected it, he could reverse the bad luck his troops had been having. He targeted Trenton, New Jersey, where a large regiment of Hessians was spending the winter.

One American soldier in Washington's battle-torn regiments predicted in his journal that Washington's plan might work. "They make a great deal of Christmas in Germany, and no doubt the Hessians will drink a great deal of beer and have a dance tonight. They will be sleepy tomorrow morning. Washington will set the tune for them about daybreak."

Col. Johann Rall was commanding the Hessians in Trenton. On Christmas night, Rall was at a party in Trenton, drinking and playing cards. His troops were in their barracks, predictably full and sleepy after a day of celebration.

A soldier handed Colonel Rall a note from a New Jersey farmer—a Loyalist. The farmer had seen evidence that the Continental army was moving toward Trenton. However, Rall did not even read the note. He stuffed it into a shirt pocket and went on with his card game.

The Battle of Trenton

Meanwhile, Washington and his troops were preparing to cross the icy Delaware River. They were going to leave the safety of Pennsylvania and return to British-held territory in New Jersey.

At various crossing points, twenty-four-hundred Americans were shivering in their thin coats as the boats zigzagged back and forth across the river. Washington had hoped that the crossing would be done by midnight, but the wind and bad weather were pushing the schedule back at least four hours.

When the men and their equipment were finally in New Jersey, there was a long nine-mile march into Trenton. As they

Washington and his troops attempt the crossing of the Delaware.

began their march, the weather turned even worse. Hail and sleet tore at the men's faces, and the biting wind battered their raggedy clothes. Washington knew his troops were freezing, and he understood that they were depressed. He trotted his grey horse up and down the column of soldiers shouting words of encouragement to them and calling them "my brave soldiers" and "my good fellows."

By the time they arrived at Trenton, most of the soldiers discovered, to their dismay, that their gunpowder was wet. Their muskets would be useless, the officers reported to Washington. The commander's answer was simple. "Use the bayonet," he replied. "I am resolved to take Trenton."

The battle was as one-sided as the battle in Long Island, New York, had been, except that this time the Continental army was in control. The Hessians were confused, and many of them ran away. Rall led the remaining force to an apple orchard outside of town and tried to mount a defense, but it was too late. Rall himself was wounded, and the Hessian battle line crumbled.

Scores of Hessians were killed, and over nine hundred were taken prisoner by the Continental army. When General Rall's men removed his shirt, they found the note that he had not read. They showed the note to Rall, who said as he lay close to death, "Had I read it when it was delivered, I would not be where I now am."

Before leaving Trenton, Washington did what was considered the gentlemanly thing to do. He paid a sick call on Colonel Rall. It seems odd in modern times that such politeness could exist in times of war, but it did. And it did not matter whether one had won or lost the battle—courtesies were still important.

For example, after one battle in Pennsylvania in which the British pounded the American army, a dog was discovered in the American camp. Two soldiers noticed that the animal had a collar with General Howe's name as the owner. The next day, an American soldier, holding a white flag in one hand and leading the dog with the other, walked over to the British lines and returned the dog. The soldier carried a note to General Howe as well, which read:

> General Washington's compliments to General Howe— does himself the pleasure to return to him a dog, which accidentally fell into his hands, and, by the inscription on the collar, appears to belong to General Howe.

Washington's surprise attack on the redcoats at the Battle of Trenton was a complete success for the American general (below). Colonel Rall surrenders to Washington after the battle (bottom).

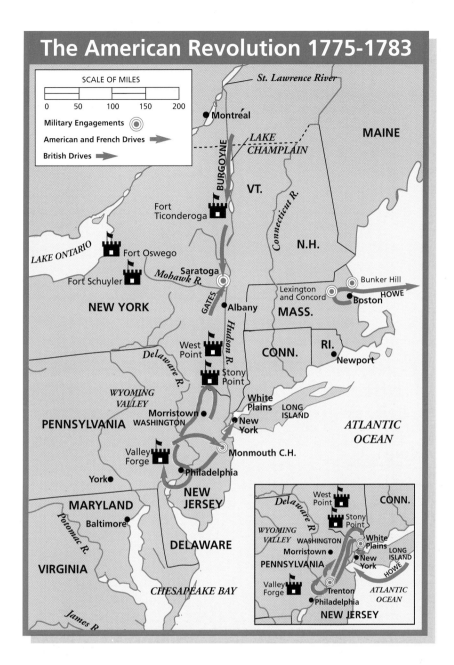

The American Revolution 1775-1783

SCALE OF MILES

0   50   100   150   200

Military Engagements

American and French Drives

British Drives

Biting the Bullet

But these moments of civilized behavior in the war were certainly the exception, not the rule. For most soldiers, the conditions of the war were a nightmare.

It may seem strange, for example, that soldiers feared dying in the war far less than being wounded. This was because medical care was primitive—today seeming downright cruel.

In most battles, there were no hospitals available. Those who survived a wound were usually cared for by friends or an overworked doctor who traveled with the troops. But the doctor

The First National Bestseller

There is a famous saying, "The pen is mightier than the sword." It is certainly true in the case of Thomas Paine during the Revolutionary War. "I know not," said John Adams in 1806, "whether any man in the world has had more influence on its inhabitants or affairs for the last thirty years than Thomas Paine."

Paine was an Englishman who had come to America in 1774 at the age of thirty-eight. He had been unsuccessful at several business attempts in England and was penniless in 1774. He enjoyed writing and talking about ideas and had gained the friendship of Benjamin Franklin, then in London. Franklin urged him to move to America and wrote Paine several letters of recommendation.

Paine found America an exciting, energizing place to live. He admired the patriotic spirit growing in the American colonies. He began writing essays about ideas he had—equal rights for people, independence, and the evils of slavery.

In January 1776, he published many of these ideas in a forty-two-page booklet called *Common Sense*. To Paine, it seemed obvious—a matter of common sense—that King George, whom Paine referred to as "the Royal Brute," had no right to rule the American people three thousand miles away. It was only right for the people of America to stand up against England.

"I cannot see," Paine wrote, "on what grounds the King of Britain can look up to heaven for help against us: a common murderer, a highwayman or a house-breaker has as good a pretence as he."

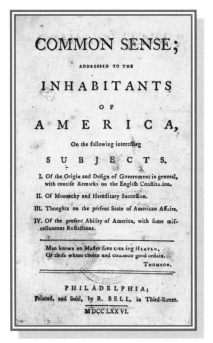

Thomas Paine's pamphlet became instantly popular among early Americans. Paine's eloquent defense for an independent and democratic United States rallied many colonists to support the Revolution.

"Everything that is right or reasonable," Paine went on, "pleads for separation. The blood of the slain, the weeping voice of nature cries, ''tis time to part.'"

Common Sense was instantly popular. Most Americans could read, and they read Paine's ideas with fervor. More than 120,000 copies were printed and sold in less than three months. On every street corner, in every tavern and store, people crowded around while they listened to someone reading Paine's essays.

Washington urged those of his soldiers who could read well to read the essays aloud to the rest of the troops. During the darkest, most pessimistic moments of the war, Paine's words were uplifting to the men. "These are the times that try men's souls," Paine wrote. "The summer soldier and the sunshine patriot will, in this crisis, shrink from the service of their country; but he that stands it now deserves the love and the thanks of man and woman."

Paine's work also had a strong effect on colonists who had before been undecided about whether to fight the British. They were moved by Paine's words and joined the patriots' cause. The last page of *Common Sense* was especially moving. There were only seven words, written in bold, black letters: "The Free and Independent States of America." Those words lit a flame in many colonists' imaginations. Liberty, they decided, was worth fighting for.

was not a respected member of the regiment, and he was looked upon with fright and suspicion.

"The doctor here is a strange fellow," wrote one young soldier in his journal. "He gives us concerns, for we are unwilling to show him our wounds. I think I would call for my friend William should I be shot, though he is but a carpenter."

Ironically, many of the doctors of that day were very similar to carpenters. They used saws, drills, and clamps just as a carpenter did. The doctors in the eighteenth century had not yet learned about infections or germs and about the necessity of keeping wounds clean. In fact, most did not wash their hands until after an operation.

The operations were unlike anything today. A soldier with a bullet in his leg had good reason to be frightened. No drugs existed that would kill the pain, so the doctor relied on four or five other soldiers to hold the wounded man down. Often the pain and panic were so intense that more assistants were needed to hold the man down.

When the doctor started working, a bullet was frequently put between the patient's teeth, a process from which we get the phrase "biting the bullet." During an operation, biting the bullet prevented the patient from biting off his tongue or lower lip, for the pain was excruciating.

No sharp, delicate instruments were used. The doctor probed for a bullet with long forceps or simply used his fingers. Wounds to legs and arms were "treated" most often by simply sawing off the limb, usually with a regular carpenter's saw. Wounds that were deep or in hard-to-reach places like the back or stomach were simply ignored. Those unlucky soldiers were simply left to bleed to death or to die of pain.

Cat and Mouse

As the fighting between the patriots and the redcoats went on in Pennsylvania and New York through 1777, the British continued to be frustrated. Although they were able to win battles, they could not deliver the "knockout punch" that would end the war.

General Howe had thought he had the perfect solution when he attacked Philadelphia in October 1777. Philadelphia had become the capital of the colonies soon after the fighting had begun at Lexington and Concord. It was the place where the Continental Congress met and made so many important decisions. Surely, Howe thought, the Revolution would crumble if Philadelphia fell.

The British took Philadelphia, but it did not finish the war. The congress quickly moved west to the little town of York, which became the new capital of the colonies.

The Revolution could not die with any one battle. Washington knew what Howe and the rest of the British failed to understand about the patriots. The desire for independence was stronger than the British army. No defeat would change their minds and make the Americans return to the role of colonists again.

So Washington cared little that he was avoiding battle. He spent months marching his army around the Northeast, staying away from a direct confrontation with General Howe's army. When Washington did attack, it was lightning-fast guerrilla warfare. He struck and ran away. This style of fighting infuriated the British.

One redcoat whose regiment spent a lot of time chasing Washington around Pennsylvania and New York wrote a letter home to his family complaining about Washington's tactics. "I don't doubt but the people have expected that we had killd & eat Washington & his whole Army long before this; But I must let you into one secret which is that they always beat us in *heels,* and in this Country there is no forcing people to fight against their Inclination."

Washington did not care a bit about showing the British his heels or that the British thought his actions "cowardly and irregular." This is how he kept his army—and the Revolution—alive.

On October 17, 1777, six thousand British troops surrendered to Gen. Horatio Gates (below) after the Battle of Saratoga (bottom).

A Turning Point

The turning point of the war occurred, oddly enough, far from Washington's army. It happened in upstate New York in a town called Saratoga. On October 17, 1777, British general John Burgoyne and six thousand of his troops surrendered to American general Horatio Gates.

Burgoyne's army had come down from Canada. He had hoped that his army could isolate the New England colonies, cutting them off from support from the other colonies. With help from two other regiments, including Clinton's army from New York City, Burgoyne wanted to confuse the Americans, who were not ready for such an attack.

At first it seemed as if his plan might succeed. But poor communication among the three attacking forces of the British army allowed the Americans time to prepare a defense. Burgoyne had waited for support from Clinton, but it never came. "At no time did the Jews await the coming of the Messiah with greater expectations than we awaited the coming of General Clinton," mourned Burgoyne in his journal.

The Americans were able to slow Burgoyne's progress and finally to surround his army. He surrendered to General Gates, who three days afterward wrote to his wife, "If Old England is not by this lesson taught humility, then she is an obstinate old slut, bent upon her ruin."

Gen. John Burgoyne surrenders to General Gates after suffering a humiliating defeat at Saratoga.

Besides the obvious advantages of wiping out a large part of the enemy's fighting force, the victory at Saratoga had another, greater importance. It brought France into the war.

Since 1775, when the fighting began, France had been watching the war with interest. France and Britain had long been rivals in Europe, and anything that weakened one benefited the other. France had sent aid secretly to the Americans but was unwilling to publicly ally itself with the Americans in the event they should lose.

But after Saratoga, the French believed in the Continental army. They formally recognized the new United States of America and signed an alliance in 1778 promising to help the United States in its war against Britain. France promised to send ships, weapons, ammunition, cash, and even military advisors to America.

"A National Disgrace"

Whatever cheer Washington's army felt hearing the news of Saratoga did not last long. The ten-thousand-man army was at the point of collapse, and Washington knew it was time to move them to winter quarters. There was little hope that Washington's army would survive the winter of 1777–1778.

The British army was still firmly entrenched in Philadelphia. Washington wanted to quarter his men near enough to keep an eye on the enemy. Valley Forge, a windy plain twenty-two miles from Philadelphia, seemed a strategic choice for a place for winter quarters.

But what might have seemed a fine location on a map was almost impossible in reality. The march alone was too much for many of the men. Washington's army was hardly even an army any longer—it was more a collection of sick, hungry, cold, ill-clothed men. Almost one-third of the men marching through the snow to Valley Forge were barefoot. Washington wrote in his journal that "you might have tracked the army…to Valley Forge by the blood of their feet."

The coats, pants, boots, and socks they had worn were threadbare after months of fighting and marching. The men were dirty, and their hair and bodies stank. Lice were everywhere, and all the men complained of "this tormenting itch." Others were ill with pneumonia and smallpox.

Washington was furious that more supplies could not reach his men. He understood that part of the problem was the very fact that the United States was a new nation. There were no systems for transporting large amounts of supplies from the seaports and cities of the East Coast on a regular basis. Things were not yet so well organized.

But Washington also knew there was another reason for the lack of supplies—greed. Many American businesspeople were making huge profits by withholding food and clothing from the army supply staff until the price went up. Historians have called the episode of Valley Forge "the lowest part of being an American—the most flagrant example of national shame."

Such profiteering, as it was called, enraged Washington. He wrote to the Continental Congress himself saying that such profiteers should hang. "No punishment in my opinion is too great for the man who can build his greatness upon his country's ruin," Washington wrote.

Those of Washington's men who were still strong enough to work were busy those first weeks at Valley Forge. There were trees to cut down and cabins to build, for Valley Forge had no buildings ready for the army—nothing except snow, cold, and a fierce wind.

Washington's troops try to survive the winter of 1777 at Valley Forge. The troops were vastly underfed, undersupplied, and ill-clothed. Some of the suffering of the soldiers was due to the greed of American businesspeople.

Unrest in the Continental Army

Many people think of the soldiers of the Continental army as patriotic, unselfish men who never lost sight of their mission. But they were human, and many made mistakes for very understandable reasons.

By 1780, the Continental soldiers had become discouraged and angry. They had been asked to fight but had not been paid except in the almost worthless Continental dollars being minted by the colonies. (Each dollar bought less than a penny's worth of goods.) And food, clothing, and other goods supposedly sent to the troops never seemed to arrive.

One private from New Jersey wrote in his journal that he saw men roasting their shoes over a fire and eating them. He also complained that he had not eaten anything in four days except for "a little black birch bark," which he gnawed off a small stick of wood. As the months went on and the soldiers continued to suffer, trouble began brewing in the ranks.

Things exploded in an ugly way in 1780. Troops in the Pennsylvania Line regiment began attacking civilians. They took money, food, valuables—anything that could be sold. Their officers tried to control the men, but they were beyond control. They even killed three of the officers sent to restore order.

Washington was frustrated. Finally, when a smaller regiment from New Jersey mutinied, he became angry. Washington ordered the ringleaders shot and warned the rest that they, too, were in danger. The action startled many and stopped the growing movement toward disobedience.

Washington and Lafayette survey the miserable conditions of the Continental army. The troops never had enough to eat.

Men took turns working. One soldier recalled later how men in thin socks would stand in their hats while on guard duty. Often groups of soldiers would pool their raggedy clothes and give them to the one who had to be on duty outdoors so he did not freeze.

The soldiers never had enough to eat. Christmas dinner that year was a few mouthfuls of rice with a tablespoon of vinegar. And the horses fared no better than the men. There was no fodder for them, and more than fifteen hundred starved that winter. By the time the coldest weather had passed, more than one-fourth of Washington's army had died of cold, malnutrition, or disease at Valley Forge. The devastating losses should have ensured that Washington's army would abandon the fight, but the army hung on. Through starvation, cold, and hardship, the army was united in the fight.

The Coming of von Steuben

In the early part of 1778, Europeans began arriving in America to help the patriots in their fight. Many Europeans had heard of the Revolution, and some were excited about the idea of helping a young country in its struggle for freedom.

One old man who came from Europe was Baron Friedrich von Steuben, and it was rumored that he had fought under the legendary king of Prussia, Frederick the Great. Von Steuben was no longer a soldier, but he was a master of precision drills. Precision drills help an army to move together at the same time by being able to respond to a general's verbal commands like

Baron Friedrich von Steuben (below) was a master at precision drills. Von Steuben is credited with drilling the Continental army (bottom) until they were able to listen and respond to verbal commands.

"left march" and "right face." Washington had never had time to train his troops rigorously in the art of obeying such drill commands.

So the Continental army had never really learned to act together. This weakness was one Washington knew made the army vulnerable to enemy fire. Fighting Indian-style—shooting from behind rocks and trees—was appropriate sometimes, but the life of his army might someday depend on the ability to obey precision commands. When von Steuben offered to teach the army these skills, Washington was overjoyed.

Von Steuben began by working with a small group of soldiers, going through basic maneuvers like about-face, standing at attention, and marching. He also taught them the secret of correctly using a bayonet, an art at which Hessians and British troops were frighteningly skilled.

Von Steuben was gruff and unpleasant. He swore at the soldiers in German, in French, and in a combination of languages. He was at first appalled at the lack of discipline in Washington's

The Battle of Monmouth (right, below) ended in a stalemate between British and American troops. But it could be considered a victory for the Americans, who proved to the British that they were a force to be reckoned with.

army. But the task of training them intrigued him. He wrote later that "in Prussia, you say to your soldier, 'Do this,' and he does it, but here I am obliged to say, 'This is the reason why you ought to do that,' and then he does it."

As grouchy as von Steuben was, the men respected him, and they learned. When his small group had been put through their paces, they went back to their regiments and taught others. By the time spring had come to Valley Forge, Washington's army had a new look. They were still raggedy, although Washington's angry letter to the Continental Congress did speed shipments of supplies a little. The change was in the men themselves. They were confident, and they looked more like a real army.

The British were in for trouble.

On Hold

Washington was eager to try out his newly trained army against Howe and the redcoats. But ironically, the two armies had little chance to cross swords. With France entering the war on the side of the Americans, Britain knew that the war would be on a larger scale.

For the British strategist in London, Lord Germain, it was important to change Britain's priorities. No longer would the British chase Washington's army around North America hoping for a decisive battle. Germain realized the British were unwittingly helping Washington's army avoid a knockout blow.

Too, the French were eager to fight the British on all fronts, not just in America. The century-long animosity between the French and British might be fought in European waters or even in the Bahamas, where the British had valuable colonial holdings. Having decided to go to war, the French might decide to try to strip Britain of the rich sugar islands in the Bahamas that it controlled.

Lord Germain in London did not know where the fighting would take place, but he knew that the current strategy was not working. He sent word to the new commander, Sir Henry Clinton, that some troops should be sent south to establish a strong front there. In case British troops were needed to fight in the Bahamas, they could be mobilized by ship from a southern port.

Washington's forces did engage the British in a battle near Monmouth, New Jersey, on June 28, 1778. Both sides were strong, and the fight ended in a stalemate. However, the battle at Monmouth sent a very clear message to the British: Washington's Continental army was a force to be reckoned with. The army had learned from their drills at Valley Forge and were capable of challenging the British troops.

The battle at Monmouth was the last time the northern armies would fight during the war. From 1778 on, the war would be fought on other fronts.

CHAPTER FOUR

The War at Sea

From the beginning of the war at Lexington and Concord, British ships silently moved along the coast of the New England colonies. Every so often, they would lob cannonballs at towns and cities along the American shore. Homes and businesses were being destroyed, and Americans were frightened. No one knew where or when the big guns would be fired again.

Although the British knew that they could not win the war with their ships, they were certain that their presence offshore could make the colonists nervous—a kind of eighteenth-century terrorism.

John Paul Jones, a sea captain recruited by Benjamin Franklin, used terrorist tactics to hassle British ships.

The Need for Sea Power

Certainly the only way to drive the ships away was for the Americans to use sea power, too. Even a few warships, they hoped, might deter the British from their indiscriminate attacks.

The colonists knew that a few warships might be able to seize British ships and cut off British supply lines. The British were fighting a war three thousand miles from their shores. In order to continue the fight, every bit of ammunition and every soldier had to be sent to North America by ship. The naval support system was the only thing keeping the British army alive. As long as the seas were clear, the British could keep sending men and supplies.

If American ships could mount a threat to the British, breaking the lifeline between the British troops and their homeland, the colonists knew they had a chance of winning the war.

But if would be a formidable task.

The Finest in the World

At the time of the Revolutionary War, the British navy was the largest, most experienced, and best-trained navy in the world. "All the oceans are a British lake," bragged a London newspaper, "and so the realm has nothing to fear from them but wind and fierce fish!"

Half of the Royal navy was made up of monstrous vessels called ships-of-the-line. They were slow and clumsy and difficult to maneuver. However, with a minimum of sixty-four cannons—and sometimes up to one hundred—a ship-of-the-line was almost indestructible.

The British had faster, lighter ships, too. These were called frigates, and they carried between thirty and forty cannons on board. Frigates acted as the lookouts of a British convoy; they escorted the larger ships.

A ship-of-the-line in the British navy carried about nine hundred men. Some of these were sailors who were needed to get the ship from one place to another. Part of the crew was made up of fighting men, whose job began once an enemy ship was sighted.

In 1775, there were 270 warships in the British navy. The Americans lacked the money needed to buy and equip more than a handful of ships. But Washington strongly believed that some sort of American navy, even a tiny one, was necessary to defeat the British. Early in the war, he announced to Congress, "The navy must have the casting vote."

The Birth of the Continental Navy

On October 30, 1775, the Continental Congress created the Continental navy. It was a modest beginning; Congress purchased four used merchant vessels and had them outfitted with cannons. Congress also raised the money to build thirteen frigates. For the new navy to have a ship-of-the-line was out of the question because the large ships were simply too expensive.

Benjamin Franklin was an important contributor in the Continental navy's beginnings. Franklin was able to buy French ships and have them equipped for war. Franklin was also instrumental in recruiting able sea captains from Europe who were interested in helping the new navy fight the British. In fact, the most famous American naval hero was one of Franklin's recruits. He was a Scotsman named John Paul Jones.

The last name "Jones" was tacked on when John Paul came to America. He had sailed on merchant vessels as a young man. Once his crew had committed mutiny, using force to overthrow him. It is said that in self-defense, John Paul used his sword to kill the ringleader of the mutiny.

The *Turtle*

There were many interesting designs for privateering ships—including an underwater boat.

While he was a student at Yale University, a young man named David Bushnell built the world's first submarine. The vessel was called the *Turtle,* and it operated by a hand-cranked propeller. According to one eyewitness, "The machine could be propelled at the rate of about three miles an hour in still water."

On the submarine was an egg-shaped explosive magazine containing 130 pounds of gunpowder that the submarine pilot could attach to an enemy vessel.

Bushnell was a frail man and felt unsure about being the one to give the *Turtle* its first taste of battle. Instead, an army sergeant named Ezra Lee took the submarine under the waters of New York Harbor in August 1776. The mission—to sink a British warship anchored there.

The mission took place late at night. The submarine was towed close to the British fleet by two whaling boats. Lee battled strong tides only to find that he was unable to attach the magazine to the British ship.

Although the mission was not successful, the *Turtle* made it to shore safely.

John Paul was worried that he might be convicted of murder. Interestingly, had he been a warship captain at the time, Jones would not have had to answer to anyone for killing a crew member. In the eighteenth century, warship captains had the power to discipline harshly, even to kill a disobedient crew member.

But John Paul's ship was a civilian vessel, so he did not have such power. Rather than take the chance that he would be convicted of murder in the trial, he took Franklin's suggestion and moved to America. He added Jones to his name, hoping to throw his pursuers off his trail.

The Most Famous American Sailor

Benjamin Franklin had urged Jones to go to Philadelphia and meet with John Adams. Adams served on the Congressional Committee for the Continental Navy and helped Jones get hired as an officer.

Adams was as impressed as Franklin with Jones's confidence and quiet strength. "His voice is soft and still and small," said Adams, "and his eye has keenness and Wildness…in it."

Jones was eager to prove his worth to the Americans. And, wisely, the young navy allowed Jones freedom to choose his own style of fighting. He and his crew waged a war of terror against the British—not in the coastal waters off America, but near England. He sailed back and forth in the English Channel, firing cannons at ships in port. When British ships gave chase, he fled to the safety of French ports.

Jones knew he could not defeat the British. But he could be a pest, an annoyance. The British could not ignore him, for he did damage that cost them time and money to repair.

Jones's most famous victory over the British took place on September 23, 1779, in the North Sea. The French had supplied him with an old merchant ship, which he refurbished, equipped with forty cannons, and named *Bonhomme Richard.* It was named after Jones's friend Benjamin Franklin. *Bonhomme Richard* means "Poor Richard" in French, and Franklin had written *Poor Richard's Almanac*—a best-selling book in Europe and America.

The *Bonhomme Richard* had three smaller ships sailing with her when one night they came upon a British convoy bringing supplies to the redcoats in America. The biggest ship in the convoy was the *Serapis.* One sailor remembered the British ship as "bristling with cannon and all sorts of guns." The two forces quickly engaged in battle.

Throughout the first hours of the sea battle, the *Serapis* was an easy winner due both to its superior weapons and to an accident. Two of the largest guns on the *Bonhomme Richard* jammed and backfired, killing many of the crew members.

The *Serapis* took advantage of the *Richard's* troubles, blasting the American ship until Jones and his crew had only three big guns left.

But the Americans fought on. As the two ships neared one another, Jones directed they be tied together, so that his crew and the British could engage in hand-to-hand combat.

In anticipation of this type of fighting the captains of the warships had made certain gruesome preparations. Jones had ordered that the walls and decks of the *Bonhomme Richard* be painted bright red so that blood would not be as frightening to the sailors once it began flowing. Both captains also ordered their sailors to throw coarse sand on the decks. The sand would soak up the blood and make the wooden decks less slippery.

The fighting between the *Serapis* and the *Bonhomme Richard* was violent. One young sailor on the *Serapis* recalled later that the "blood and gruesome remains of fellows was ankle-deep in places on the decks."

Nathaniel Fanning, a young midshipman from Connecticut, remembered the weapons the fighting sailors used:

> The battle was renewed with redoubled vigour, with what cannon we could manage, hand grenades, stink pots [buckets filled with rotten fish or sulphur set on fire] but principally, towards the closing scene, with lances and boarding pikes. With these the combatants killed each other through the ships port holes.

The Bonhomme Richard, *named after Benjamin Franklin's* Almanack *(below), battles with the* Serapis *(bottom).*

Poor Richard, 1733.
AN
Almanack
For the Year of Chrift
1733,
Being the Firft after LEAP YEAR:

And makes fince the Creation — Years
By the Account of the Eastern *Greeks* — 7241
By the Latin Church, when ☉ ent. ♈ — 6932
By the Computation of *W. W.* — 5742
By the *Roman* Chronology — 5682
By the *Jewish* Rabbies — 5494

Wherein is contained
The Lunations, Eclipfes, Judgment of the Weather, Spring Tides, Planets Motions & mutual Afpects, Sun and Moon's Rifing and Setting, Length of Days, Time of High Water, Fairs, Courts, and obfervable Days.
Fitted to the Latitude of Forty Degrees, and a Meridian of Five Hours Weft from *London*, but may without fenfible Error, ferve all the adjacent Places, even from *Newfoundland* to *South-Carolina*.

By *RICHARD SAUNDERS*, Philom.

PHILADELPHIA:
Printed and fold by *B. FRANKLIN*, at the New Printing-Office near the Market.

John Paul Jones refused to give up until he had captured and boarded the Serapis *(right, above). Shouting, "I have not yet begun to fight," Jones rallied his beleaguered crew, forcing the* Serapis *to strike its colors.*

"I Have Not Yet Begun to Fight!"

The *Bonhomme Richard* was on fire, and many of its crew were dead. One American sailor began screaming, "Quarter, quarter!"—meaning that he felt it was time to surrender. Jones reportedly broke the man's skull with the butt of his pistol.

Jones did not want to give up. In fact, when the captain of the *Serapis* asked Jones if he planned to "strike his colors," or remove his flag in a gesture of surrender, witnesses say that Jones scoffed. "I have not yet begun to fight!," he cried.

Those words invigorated his tired crew. The Americans were able, after more than three hours of fighting, to use homemade bombs to set off explosions in the kegs of British gunpowder. The *Serapis* finally struck its colors, and the battle was over.

The *Bonhomme Richard* was so badly damaged that it sank after a few hours. Jones and his crew took command of the *Serapis* and brought her and her crew to port. From this battle, Jones established himself as the first hero of the American navy. In fact, the words "I have not yet begun to fight" became the navy motto.

Birth of the Privateers

But even with such heroics, the British eventually defeated the Continental navy. The Royal navy simply outnumbered the Americans. Within a few months of Jones's victory over the *Serapis,* British shipbuilders were turning out scores of new vessels—poorly made, for materials were too expensive for the depressed British economy, but they could float. Large British fleets bottled up the harbors so that American ships could not sail.

However, this was not the end of American naval battles. A new force took over—one that was not run by the American government. Hundreds of private citizens used their own ships to join the war effort. The owners equipped the ships with cannons and guns, and the vessels were ready for battle. These privateers, as they were called, hired their own crews. The crews were paid in prize money. When a privateer seized a British ship, he took its cargo to the nearest port and sold it. The money was then divided among the crew.

Captains of privateering vessels had no trouble recruiting sailors. The average family in America in 1777 got by on less than fifteen dollars monthly. A privateer could make more than one thousand dollars in just one British prize.

A colonist from Massachusetts, Ebenezer Fox, wrote in his journal that when a recruiting officer "espied any large boys among the idle crowd crowded around him he would attract their attention by singing in a comical manner:

> All you that have bad Masters,
> And cannot get your due,
> Come, come, my brave boys
> And join our ship's crew!

"Shouting and huzzahing would follow," wrote Fox, "and some join the ranks."

Not Without Risk

Yet privateering, for all of its promise of wealth, was not without risk. British warships captured many American sailors. They were not, technically, in the armed forces, so they could not be treated as prisoners of war. However, the British were reluctant to hang them as pirates for fear that British prisoners would be hanged in turn.

The British solution was to keep captured American seamen in the most miserable, wretched conditions imaginable. The British used large old ships called hulks and converted them to prisons. The British stripped them of sails and fittings and boarded up portholes. There were small slits cut in the ships' sides for air, but otherwise the prisoners were completely sealed in.

Quakers

Most privateering vessels were nowhere near as well armed as British ships. Ship cannons and other artillery were too expensive for most privateers to purchase. Besides, privateering vessels were built in secret in out-of-the-way bays along the coast. A large order of weapons in town might alert redcoats or Tory spies, which would be dangerous to the privateers.

Instead, the privateering captain had to rely on speed, the element of surprise, and deceit. One of the favorite means of tricking British sea captains was the use of quakers. A quaker was actually a log that had been smoothed and shaped to look like a cannon. For a final touch, the privateers would blacken the log to make it look like the real thing.

Although quakers could not be fired, they could pass for cannons at a distance. A shipful of yelling, cursing privateers on a ship bristling with what appeared to be cannons was often enough for a British captain to turn and run.

Quakers were far cheaper than real cannons, too. In 1780, a privateer could purchase one for about twelve pounds. A pair of real four-pound guns would sell for twenty-five hundred pounds.

The jail hulk Old Jersey. *Americans would rather die than be captured and placed on these filthy, rat-infested ships where many soldiers died of disease and starvation. More than thirteen thousand American soldiers died aboard these floating prisons.*

The hulks were ghastly, filthy places. Hundreds of men were crowded into rooms that would be cramped quarters for twenty. When they received any food at all, it was rotten and crawling with insects. Their water was, according to prisoners who survived, "an astonishing greenish-yellow, which had a foul, sour smell."

Rats were everywhere, and with the rats came disease. Smallpox, yellow fever, and severe diarrhea were common. And because the prisoners were cramped so close together, the disease spread quickly.

At the age of eighteen, young Thomas Andros was captured by the British and sent to the hulk *Old Jersey*. He recalled how the first thing prisoners heard each morning was the command from the guards, "Rebels, turn out your dead!" The Americans then hoisted up the bodies of the men who had died during the night.

According to Andros, prisoners were allowed to ascend to the deck in the morning. "But the first object that met our view in the morning," wrote Andros later, "was a most appalling spectacle—a boat loaded with dead bodies, conveying them to the Long Island shore, where they were very slightly covered with sand.... Let our disease be what it would, we were abandoned to our fate."

The prison ships killed more than thirteen thousand Americans during the war. The *Old Jersey* was known as the worst. Eleven thousand men—more than the total killed in George Washington's army—died aboard that ship, known as "Hell Afloat."

Putting Pressure on Britain

The success of the privateers who avoided the hulks is legendary. The two thousand privately owned American ships carried over seventy thousand men into battle during the years of the Revolutionary War. The privateers captured and brought in almost three thousand British ships, most of them merchant vessels.

The value of these ships paid a total of $50 million in prize money to the privateers and their crews. Most of these captured supplies were brought to American coastal towns, where they were sold to supply officers for George Washington's troops.

Although American sea power was limited, it had its desired effect. British ships could no longer sail at will between England and the colonies. There was always at least a threat that they might meet up with an armed American vessel. And British merchants began pressing their government to put an end to the war. The millions of dollars of cargo they were losing to the American privateers was, they insisted, too high a price to pay for keeping the "traitorous Rebels" in line.

But the British military was far from giving up the fight. Ironically, the British would use a new enemy to fight the American forces. This new enemy would come not from Europe, but from the United States' own frontier.

CHAPTER FIVE

The Frontier on Fire

In 1763, long before the war broke out, King George had issued a proclamation to the American colonists telling them not to move any farther west than the Allegheny Mountains. Native Americans, angry because the white settlers were taking over their territory with farms and homes, had warned the settlers to turn back, and the British government took the warnings seriously.

The king knew that the Indians would declare war on the settlers who were trickling in greater and greater numbers over the mountains. King George also knew it would be very hard—and expensive—to fight such a war against the Indians. It would be best, he decided, to avoid confrontation.

An Easy Alliance

But many Americans paid no attention to the proclamation. They were determined to move. Led by pioneers like Daniel Boone, Americans who loved adventure—or who hated the crowded conditions in the East—came to the unexplored lands just over the Alleghenies.

But the Indians watched with growing concern. Settlers cut down trees, made roads, and cleared land for farms. The settlers were threatening the Indian way of life.

The Indians were angry, and the British saw a way to take advantage of the situation. When war broke out, British officials met with Indian leaders. They encouraged the Indians to fight the settlers and even gave the Indians money and weapons.

Terrorism on the Frontier

The British hoped the Indians would make the settlers so nervous and fearful that they would urge the government to end the fighting.

The British made no secret of their actions. William Tryon, a British general, claimed that Britain's plan was to "loose the savages against the miserable Rebels in order to impose a reign of terror on the frontier."

Indian raids on settlements were lightning fast. They would surprise the settlers and run away. If the settlers had been warned and were ready for a fight, the Indians would simply vanish among the trees.

One of the most feared Indian customs in warfare was scalping, a practice learned centuries before from the Spanish who came to America. Many Indian tribes believed that the soul of a person was in the hair on his or her head. By using a knife to cut off the hair and skin at the top of the skull, Indians believed they were taking their enemy's spirit. There would be no way that the person's ghost could seek revenge later.

Many Indians collected and displayed the scalps they took. The scalps were dried on little frames and later worn on an Indian brave's leather belt. They were like war medals, and each one had a story that could be related over and over again.

Native Americans were concerned and angry as settlers took over their territory and moved farther west. British soldiers tried to exploit this anger by inciting the Indians to fight against the U.S. colonists.

Scalping was not the only thing the settlers feared about an Indian attack. Many Indian tribes tortured their prisoners. Some tribes tortured prisoners to give them the chance to show their courage. The list of ways settlers were tortured, however, makes it hard to believe anyone could stand up to such pain.

For instance, when a soldier named Colonel Clark was captured by Delaware Indians, he was put through incredible pain. He was made to wear a necklace of red-hot tomahawks, he was forced to walk barefoot on hot coals, and he was made to run through two lines of club-swinging Indian braves. (The last was called "running the gauntlet.") But his punishment did not end there, according to a fellow officer who witnessed it all before escaping:

> Some little time after they scalped him and struck him on the bare skull several times with sticks. Being now nearly exhausted, he lay down on the burning embers, when the squaws put shovels full of coals on his body, which, dying as he was, made him move and creep a little. The doctor [a friend of the colonel] was able to stand by and see the cruelty performed. When the colonel was scalped, they slapped the scalp over the doctor's face, saying, "This is your great captain's scalp; tomorrow we will serve you so."

But the British plan backfired in a big way. The Indian attacks were so bloody and so horrible that British citizens became offended.

One of the most feared Indian practices in warfare was scalping (below). The British incited Indians to attack U.S. colonists, even paying Indians for American scalps (bottom).

Such stories astonished and horrified many British people. "What are we doing, in the name of God?" asked one member of Parliament. "We have given permission to these [Indians] to behead, to burn, to dismember our brethren in America! For what purpose, I know not!"

The terrorism also changed the opinions of many Americans who had been neither for nor against the Revolution. Some Americans who leaned toward the Loyalist position were appalled by the reports coming from the frontier. If their king was ordering such slaughter, how could he have their best interests at heart? Many of these Americans joined the patriot cause.

Directing the Violence

During the war, violence between Indians and settlers took place on two fronts. One front was the central and western parts of Pennsylvania and New York. The British controlled Indian activities in this area from Fort Niagara on Lake Ontario. The Iroquois tribes living near there fought the war with British-made supplies and ammunition.

The other front was the Northwest Territory—now the states of Kentucky and Illinois. In the eighteenth century, the northwest was different than today. Settlers had no idea how far west the land actually extended. The areas known today as California, Arizona, or even Texas were unknown to them. This little-explored land of the frontier was as far west as they could imagine.

The British offered their assistance to Indians in the Northwest Territory from headquarters at Fort Detroit, near Lake Erie. Col. Henry Hamilton was in command of the British forces there. He was known to Americans as the "Hair Buyer," for he offered money for every settler's scalp the Indians brought to him.

One young man from Kentucky was determined to fight back—not just against the Indians, but against Hair Buyer Hamilton himself. George Rogers Clark, age 25, organized a band of 170 frontiersmen in June 1778 to march against the British settlements in the Northwest Territory.

Victory Without Bloodshed

Clark and his band set off in boats from Pittsburgh and floated much of the way on the Ohio River. From the river they marched 120 miles to their first target—the British outpost called Kaskaskia in what now is southern Illinois.

Kaskaskia was held by a detachment of French soldiers who had, after the French and Indian War, pledged loyalty to King

Immoral Weapons

In the twentieth century, certain weapons are considered immoral. Interestingly enough, there were weapons considered immoral in the Revolutionary War, too. In 1775, one British officer suggested putting smallpox germs on arrowheads and shooting them at Americans. (His superior officers would not allow it.)

In the summer of 1776, British soldiers claimed that the Continental soldiers were quartering or halving musket balls. Such ammunition would fragment and rip the flesh once it hit the body. Wounds from such musket balls were more serious and far more painful than wounds from unfragmented musket balls. Surgeons would have an impossible task trying to repair the damage left to muscle and bone.

British general Howe wrote a terse note to General Washington complaining that Continentals were firing lead bullets with the points of nails protruding from them. Howe gave Washington the benefit of the doubt, as he said, "being well assured the contrivance has not come to your knowledge."

Washington replied two days later in a short letter. He claimed that a sample bullet that Howe had sent was the first he had ever seen. He called its use a "wicked and infamous practice."

George. Clark and his men were friendly and open with the French troops. The French were not sure whether they should surrender to Clark or fight.

Clark told them about the treaty France had just signed with America. When the French learned that their government was officially on the side of America, they gladly surrendered the outpost to Clark.

Clark and his forces pushed north to French-held Cahokia, and the same thing happened there. Finally, Clark sent a detachment of his men to Vincennes, in what is now southern Indiana, to occupy that fort. In a matter of days, Clark had won over three important British outposts without firing a shot.

The Coming of the Hair Buyer

At Fort Detroit, Hamilton heard the news of Clark's victories with concern. He knew that with the Americans in charge of valuable outposts, British control in the area was threatened. In October, Hamilton, together with a force of five hundred British soldiers, set out to retake Vincennes.

Clark was well aware that his control of the outposts was shaky. He could not leave a large force behind at each outpost to keep control. He did not have that many men, even with the French who had joined his forces. Instead, he had ordered a few men to stay behind at each fort, hoping there would be no immediate threat to the American position.

It is not surprising, then, that Hamilton was able to retake Vincennes quite easily in December. Clark's representatives there were taken prisoner, and once more the fort was in British hands.

An Impossible March

Meanwhile, more than 180 miles from Vincennes, Clark had a tough decision to make. His fighting force was down to about one hundred men. He knew that if Hamilton attacked him, he would surely be defeated. He and his men could turn around and head back east. Or, he could do the unexpected—attack.

It was a tremendous long shot. But Clark was confident that the element of surprise, combined with a little trickery, would throw Hamilton off guard. He pleaded with local militia in the area and was able to talk about eighty additional men into joining him.

The march to Vincennes, beginning February 6, 1779, was one of the most famous feats of the entire war. Even though it was winter, Clark's men would not have had difficulty with the

The Mighty Six Nations

The Iroquois Indians were a much-feared force on the frontier during the Revolutionary War. The Iroquois were sometimes known to the whites as the Six Nations. The Iroquois were not a tribe; rather, they were a confederation of six separate tribes—the Mohawk, Oneida, Onondaga, Cayuga, Seneca, and the Tuscaroras.

The League of the Five Nations, as the confederation was called before the Tuscaroras entered in 1722, was formed around 1450. The tribes realized they could be far more influential and powerful as a group. The Iroquois were able to defeat large tribes such as the Hurons and to take over their land. By the early eighteenth century, the Iroquois were the dominant power along the frontier in New York State.

The Iroquois called themselves the Ongwanonhsioni, which means "the keepers of the longhouses." They did, in fact, live in longhouses—one-hundred-foot-long buildings made of poles and bark. Many whites, seeing an Iroquois village for the first time, were surprised at how "civilized" they were. (Many whites believed the Indians to be savages who lived in tipis.) Some villages had clusters of more than one hundred longhouses with neatly kept gardens and play areas for children.

When war broke out in the colonies, both the British and Americans wanted the Iroquois on their sides. The war ended up fragmenting the Six Nations, however. Joseph Brant, the Mohawk leader, persuaded four of the tribes to fight for the British, while two tribes, the Oneidas and the Tuscaroras, fought for the Americans.

The Iroquois were a confederation of six tribes who had decided to form a league of nations to defeat enemy tribes. After the Revolutionary War, the league became fractured.

George Clark marches across the Wabash River, through wilderness and flood, to retake Vincennes.

wilderness march, for they were strong and hardy and used to long excursions into the wilderness. However, there had been a few springlike days, and the area had been turned into a huge lake. In some places the water was ankle deep; other places had water as high as a man's chin.

Thanks to Clark's sense of humor, the men were in good spirits most of the march. They were still on fairly high ground, and there was even enough game to shoot for dinner. However, when they were twenty miles from Vincennes, everything went wrong.

Clark and his men had come to the Little Wabash River, which had overflowed its banks. The men had to slosh through frigid water as high as their shoulders. Their arms and backs ached from holding their rifles and gunpowder high over their heads.

Game, which had been plentiful before, was now scarce. Supplies had run out. The twenty-five miles each day the group had been marching at the first part of the journey dropped to three or four. Men were growing weak and sick for lack of food and from sleeping in shallow ice water for a few hours each night. The sick were placed in canoes, and those who were strong enough pushed them through the cold water.

At last Clark and his men reached higher ground. They lit fires and warmed themselves, and that lifted their spirits once more. But bad news arrived. A passerby informed them that Hamilton's forces had grown larger. An additional two hundred Indians had come to Vincennes to join the Hair Buyer at the fort. Outnumbered before, Clark's forces now seemed to have no chance at all against Hair Buyer Hamilton.

The Old "March 'Em Around in Circles" Trick

As small as his numbers were, George Rogers Clark was able to fool Hamilton and his men. By trickery, he made the Hair Buyer believe that he had almost ten times as many men as he really had.

The way he did it was ridiculously easy. He marched his men down the main street of Vincennes. Once they were in the street, Clark divided his men into smaller bands. The two divisions swung to each side, through side streets, and doubled back to the main street. In effect, the men were marching in circles. To observers, it seemed that Clark's parade went on forever.

The townspeople, terrified of being on the losing side of a battle, immediately sided with Clark. They agreed to help him fight and even guided Clark's men to secret stashes of ammunition Hamilton had set aside.

An Important Victory

The battle for the fort was really over before it began. Hamilton, astonished by Clark's arrival, ordered his gunners to fire at the frontiersmen. But Clark's men were sharpshooters. As one of the men bragged, "It was nothing for my brother and I to shoot a squirrel in the eye from 100 yards away." Clark's frontiersmen had no trouble picking off the gunners behind the fortress wall.

By late that afternoon, Hamilton and his men surrendered. The man known as the Hair Buyer was sent to jail in Williamsburg, Virginia. Without strong British influence in the area, the frontier, once held by the British, became friendly to the United States. The lands of the Northwest Territory were won for America, thanks to George Rogers Clark and his men.

Joseph Brant

As in the Northwest Territory, the settlers along the eastern frontier were having trouble with Indians and their British allies. The fighting between Indians and settlers began before the war, and it intensified once the British became involved.

Through trickery, Clark was able to convince the British that he had far more men than they had. After Clark's sharpshooters pick off British soldiers fighting along the fort's walls (below left), Hamilton and his men surrender (below right).

Joseph Brant was fiercely loyal to the British and convinced the Iroquois alliance to also fight on the British side.

The fighting was well organized against the settlers. The British had formed a strong alliance with a respected Mohawk leader, Thayendanegea. To the whites, he was known as Joseph Brant.

Brant had been adopted as a teenager by Sir William Johnson, a British general. Brant was sent to school in Connecticut and became the first of his tribe to learn to read and write English.

A well-read, thoughtful man, Brant was invited to England during the first part of the Revolutionary War. Because his background was so different from anyone the British had met, and because he was such an intelligent, well-bred man, Brant was wined and dined as an important foreign diplomat—a much-sought-after guest at every social event.

Because of his close kinship with the British people, Brant was intensely loyal to the British cause during the war. He signed an oath of allegiance to Britain and was able to convince the Iroquois tribes, known thereafter as the Six Nations, to do the same.

Setting the Frontier Ablaze

Brant allied himself with a group of Tories known as Butler's Rangers. The Rangers had been driven out of their New York homes by patriots. John Butler and his son Walter led the group. Butler's Rangers planned to attack settlements in Pennsylvania and New York.

In July 1778, Butler's Rangers, together with Brant and his Iroquois Indian fighters, attacked the peaceful Wyoming Valley in northeastern Pennsylvania. The valley was an important place, for it supplied a great deal of the food for the people of Pennsylvania. Pennsylvanians had set up a series of little forts to defend the valley.

Brant's attack was sudden and vicious. The raiders killed whole families, even babies and small children. More than one thousand homes were burned to the ground, fields were trampled, and cattle and other livestock were shot and left to rot in the pastures.

The slaughter at Wyoming Valley was followed two months later by another at a village in the Mohawk Valley and another in the Cherry Valley in New York. Those settlers who were lucky enough to get away with their lives described the attacks as "blood-baths" and "nightmares of a kind of hell on earth."

Hideous stories of torture and slaughter reached General Washington. He was concerned not only for the settlements, but also for the security of the farmlands and the safety of his own lines of troops in the area. He knew something had to be done.

The Secret War

Military leaders of the Revolutionary War depended on information about the enemy. Professional spies were unreliable, according to George Washington, for they were so good that they "lacked the virtue to withstand the highest bidder." In other words, they had no special allegiance or loyalty and could be bribed.

Both the British and American armies had spies, agents, and couriers whose job it was to find out about enemy troop movement, kinds of weapons—anything to give their side an advantage.

Of course this information had to be delivered in person since there were no telephones, radios, or telegraphs in those days. Ordinary-appearing citizens did the delivering of secret messages—teachers, clergy, or even children slipped through enemy lines with messages.

Even if the messengers were caught, there was no guaranteeing the enemy could find anything incriminating. Secret messages were often written in codes or with invisible ink.

Washington valued his spies more than any other members of his army. "Wherever [the British] Army lies," he declared, "it will be of the greatest advantage to us to have spies among them." Washington put muscle behind his words, too. His spies were the only ones paid in "real" money—gold and silver coins. The fighting men were paid in paper money, which was worth next to nothing.

Both the British and the Americans employed spies to carry secret information about the enemy. One of the most well known of these spies was Benedict Arnold (left).

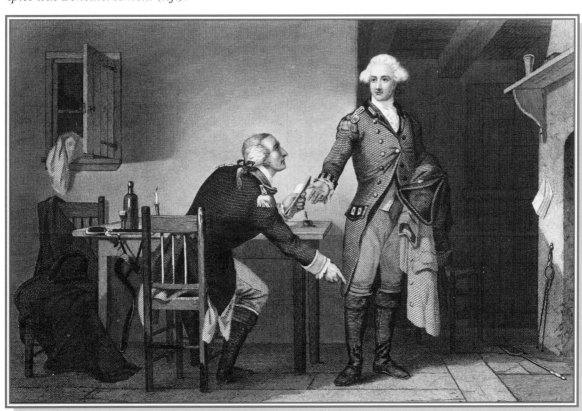

Yankee Doodle Dandy

Even before the war began, many British people looked down on the American colonists. To people in Britain, the Americans seemed like poorly educated farmers who dressed in ill-fitting clothing and lacked good manners.

The song "Yankee Doodle" was written by a British doctor who worked in America in 1758. The word "Doodle" is an English term meaning fool or simple-minded person. *Janke,* a Dutch name used by many settlers in the colonies, became the word Yankee. Therefore, a Yankee Doodle is a term of ridicule and scorn.

Many of the British soldiers who came to America to fight sang the song to mock the Continentals. However, the Americans added their own words to the song during the Revolutionary War:

Yankee Doodle is the tune
Americans delight in;
It suits for feasts, it suits for fun,
And just as well for fighting.

The song was sung at the first Fouth of July celebration in Philadelphia in 1777, just as it is included in such celebrations today.

An Eye for an Eye

The answer to the violence of the Tories and Indians turned out to be more violence. George Washington mobilized a large force of the Continental army. Led by experienced Maj. Gen. John Sullivan, their job was to cut a path of destruction all the way through the Iroquois territory. In Washington's own words, the land of the Six Nations was to be invaded "with the total destruction…of their settlements and the capture of as many prisoners…as possible."

The Continental army had two goals. The first was obvious—to destroy as much of the military force of the Tories and Iroquois as possible. But Washington also felt it was important to destroy the Indians' farmland right at the time when their crops were close to harvest. People who were hungry and had no means of feeding themselves were less likely to wage war, he reasoned.

General Sullivan set out in the early summer of 1779 with the largest military force ever assembled on the frontier—a little over four thousand men. They struck first at the Indian settlement of Chemung in New York. Chemung was a surprise to many of Sullivan's men, for it was different than they had imagined Indian

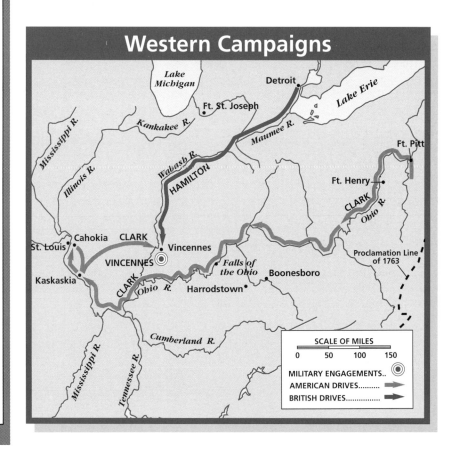

villages to be. Instead of handfuls of wigwams scattered about, there were, as one soldier wrote, "between 30 & 40 Houses, some of them large and neatly finish'd; particularly a Chapel and Council House."

The town burned quickly. The people of Chemung offered no resistance; they fled before the soldiers arrived. They must have realized they had no chance against such a large fighting force.

As Washington had specified, everything was destroyed, even animals such as chickens, geese, and farm dogs. As another soldier noted, the town caught flame in a "glorious Bonfire and wide fields of grain and vegetables were ruin'd."

The destruction went on, village after village. Most of the time, it was the same as in Chemung—the streets and farms were deserted. There was one point at which Tories and Indians did try to ambush the soldiers, but they were soundly crushed.

One soldier from New Jersey, Lt. William Barton, was especially proud of a "trophy" he acquired after the battle. He wrote later that he found many dead Indians after the fight and that he "skinned two of them from their hips down for boot legs; one pair for the Major, the other for myself." Obviously, the butchery and atrocities were not limited to the Indian warriors.

A Plan That Backfired

Although the attacks on Indian settlements were effective for a while, they were not completely successful from a military standpoint. The Indians had not been defeated—merely pushed back. In fact, by the time Sullivan's destructive raids were completed, most of the people of the Six Nations had retreated all the way back to Fort Niagara.

Their food stores were ashes, and they had no crops to harvest that year. Many Indians, especially the old and very young, died of starvation. Others became totally dependent on the British at Fort Niagara for food and supplies. This dependence created a financial strain on the British, for there were thousands of people who needed support.

And because the Indians were not destroyed, Washington's plan had backfired in another important way. Stripped of their land and food, the Indians became more fiercely loyal to the British. The Indians hated the white settlers on the frontier.

This hatred is one reason why, at the end of the Revolutionary War, long after a treaty was signed between Britain and the United States, the fighting between Indians and whites continued on the American frontier.

CHAPTER SIX

The Final Battles

By the fall of 1779, much of the fighting had ground to a halt. There were still skirmishes between Indians and settlers on the frontier, but in the East, the British army and the Continental army were playing a waiting game. The British were comfortably entrenched in New York, and Washington's army watched from a distance. Neither wanted to risk a large portion of their army in a major battle.

Win It or Come Home

In Britain there was a great deal of concern over the war effort. Many members of Parliament were angry about the astronomical cost of the war. In addition to arming and providing supplies to the redcoats, almost thirty thousand foreign mercenaries had been hired who needed to be paid and supplied. In addition, Washington's destruction of Indian supplies meant the British were feeding thousands of Indians. In a nation already riddled with financial problems from its last war, these mounting debts were too much to bear.

Many in Parliament urged the British army either to win the war quickly or return to England. Having Britain's entire army in America posed a potential threat to British security. What if they were attacked by France, or by Spain? Who would guard their shores? they wondered.

But Prime Minister Lord North and King George did not want to end the war. They thought that giving in to the colonies would make Britain look foolish to the rest of the world and would be "morally, completely unacceptable," according to Lord North. The war must be fought and won by the British. There would be no giving in.

Taking the War South

Declaring that the British would win the war was relatively easy. But the prime minister's opponents in Parliament were persistent. How did the king plan to win the war? What could be done that was not already being done?

The answer from Lord Germain, the British military strategist in London, was simple—move the war south. Since nothing was happening in New England, and the British were having a difficult time fighting on the frontier, it was important to begin a new attack, in a new location.

There seemed to be several good reasons to begin a southern military campaign. First, the South was a financially crucial part of the colonies. The tobacco grown in the South brought in much-needed money that helped support the Continental war effort.

The South was important, too, because of the huge quantities of food grown on its farms and plantations. Just as the Tories and Iroquois hurt the patriots by destroying the Wyoming Valley farms, the British could severely hurt the colonies by taking over their food supply.

But opponents to the war in Parliament were insistent. How could such a war be won? Every available soldier was already serving in America. There were no more forces to send.

A British representative in New York came up with the answer. He claimed that there were many, many Loyalists living in the South—far more than on the frontier or in New England. The North, not the South, was for independence. The South's whole economy was based on trading with England, and Loyalists there would not want to jeopardize that. Loyalists would surely fight the patriots if the war were moved down into their territory. The British, he suggested, merely had to provide the leadership.

The prospect of a war with Americans fighting Americans was attractive to the British government and to the overworked military. Within a few weeks, the southern campaign was well underway.

Civil War Begins

The seaport of Savannah, Georgia, had been taken easily by British troops even before the southern campaign was officially underway. Without much difficulty, Gen. Henry Clinton was able to seize another important southern city—Charleston, South Carolina. This was done by May, 1780.

A Most Unusual Coincidence

In 1800, the city of Washington, D.C., replaced Philadelphia as the capital of America. A special Fourth of July celebration was to be held there in 1826, marking the fiftieth anniversary of the signing of the Declaration of Independence. Dignitaries from all over the country, especially the signers of the Declaration, were invited to participate in the celebration. Two important people could not make it.

The first was John Adams, then ninety years old. He was too old to make the trip from Massachusetts. The other was Thomas Jefferson, then eighty-three. He, too, was unable to make the journey because of failing health.

Several days after the celebration, two bits of startling news were sent to President John Quincy Adams (son of John Adams). Both Thomas Jefferson and John Adams had died—on the same day—July 4.

Some thought it was a "most unusual coincidence." Others were sure it was a sign from God that the men had died on the fiftieth anniversary of the signing of the Declaration. There was no disagreement, however, that it was a sad day for America to lose two of its most important founders.

Once the takeover of Charleston had been accomplished, Clinton went back to his headquarters in New York, leaving Gen. Charles Cornwallis in charge. It was then that the vicious civil war that the British had hoped for really began.

A regiment of the Continental army from Virginia led by Gen. Abraham Buford was on its way to Charleston. They had heard that the British were attacking the city and had come to help the patriots. As they neared Charleston, they heard the city was already in British hands, and they turned around to head north.

"Butcher" Tarleton

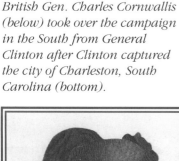

British Gen. Charles Cornwallis (below) took over the campaign in the South from General Clinton after Clinton captured the city of Charleston, South Carolina (bottom).

Buford's four-hundred-man regiment ran into trouble that day. A wild group of Tories from Pennsylvania, New York, and some southern colonies began chasing them. The group called themselves the Dragoon Guards and prided themselves on being the most bloodthirsty fighters around.

The leader of the Dragoon Guards was a twenty-six-year-old British colonel named Banastre Tarleton. Tarleton was something of a dandy who loved skin-tight clothes, colorful capes, and tall bushy hats with plumes. After this day he would be known by the Continental army as "Butcher" Tarleton.

Tarleton and his men ran at Buford's men screaming and cursing. After the first charge by Tarleton, Buford realized that his men had no chance. He ordered his army to throw down their weapons and instructed a flag bearer to walk with a white truce flag toward the attackers.

Tarleton chose to ignore the time-honored signal for truce. He screamed to his men to use their bayonets and attack the now-unarmed Continentals. "No quarter, no quarter," shouted the Dragoon Guard. (Quarter is the old term meaning "mercy.")

For the next fifteen minutes, a slaughter took place. The Dragoon Guard savagely ripped through the crowds of patriots, plunging their sharp bayonets into body after body.

A young man named Robert Brownsfield witnessed the slaughter. He later described how sickened he was by the sight of Tarleton's men stabbing dying men:

> After every man was prostrate, they went over the ground plunging their bayonets into everyone that exhibited any signs of life, and in some instances, where several had fallen one over the other, these monsters were seen to throw off on the point of the bayonet the uppermost, to come at those beneath.

More than 260 Continental soldiers were killed attempting to surrender. From that day forward, an ugly kind of warfare took over the South. Among the patriots, the phrase, "Tarleton's Quarter" became a kind of password. Many patriots in the South were eager to avenge the atrocities committed by Butcher Tarleton. Such revenge, of course, meant that they, too, began committing atrocities. Prisoners were seldom taken, and quick, on-the-spot hangings of captives were common among both the patriot and Loyalist groups.

(Below) British Col. Banastre Tarleton, typically dressed in one of the flamboyant outfits that he loved. Tarleton's infamous slaughter of unarmed American soldiers at Camden (bottom) left many southern Americans thirsty for revenge.

Marching Toward Virginia

After Tarleton's victory and a victory over the Continental army in Camden, General Cornwallis felt that South Carolina was safely in British hands. After securing the South, the British planned to "come in the back door" to Virginia. Virginia was a very important part of the Revolution. It was the largest colony, and one of the most wealthy. Too, because it was centrally located, supplies and communications between the southern Continentals and Washington's troops had to pass through Virginia. Cornwallis and other British officers felt that if they could control Virginia, they could win the war. And since it had not worked to move south from New England against Washington's troops, it hopefully would work to move north.

After the easy Camden victory, Cornwallis split his forces. The left flank was commanded by a young officer named Maj. Patrick Ferguson. As Ferguson and his troops marched toward North Carolina, they enjoyed themselves by looting and burning homes and farms belonging to patriots.

As Ferguson drew closer to the North Carolina border, he sent a message ahead to the frontiersmen who lived across the mountains—the "over-mountain men," as they were known. He told them he intended to defeat them, and if they wanted to avoid being killed and having their homes burned, they should surrender at once.

The Over-Mountain Men

The over-mountain men were a fierce, independent group of people. Most were originally from Ireland or Scotland, and they loved their remote mountain homes. They often had a hard enough time getting along with one another. But for a British soldier to threaten them, ordering them to lay down their precious long rifles and surrender—never!

Rather than surrender, they decided to attack. More than one thousand over-mountain men, led by William Campbell, went looking for Ferguson and his troops.

The over-mountain men found Ferguson's troops at King's Mountain on the border between North and South Carolina. Although Ferguson actually had two hundred more men, the battle did not go his way. The over-mountain men, in their deerskin pants and raccoon caps, had the advantage. They could shoot.

From high in the treetops growing on the mountain, the frontiersmen picked off Ferguson's men one by one. Ferguson himself tried to urge his men on. At one point he yelled that not even "God Almighty and all the rebels out of Hell" would defeat him.

As more and more of the British-Tory band fell, some of Ferguson's men began waving white flags. Ferguson angrily used his

In the Battle of King's Mountain (above and left), the over-mountain men got their revenge for Tarleton's massacre. Excellent shots, the ragged frontiersmen were able to pick off the British soldiers one by one. When the British surrendered, however, the frontiersmen murdered many of them.

sword to cut down the men who dared to surrender. Finally, Ferguson was killed by six shots, and his troops quickly surrendered.

But the over-mountain men had learned the lesson of Banastre Tarleton. They, too, could be treacherous. Yelling "Tarleton's quarter, Tarleton's quarter!" they killed the surrendering soldiers. When he saw what his men were doing, William Campbell rode his horse among them. "For God's sake, quit!" he is said to have cried. "It's murder to shoot any more!"

The one-sided battle at King's Mountain forced Cornwallis to rethink his strategy. He realized that he did not have the manpower or the control to move into North Carolina. In fact, his control of South Carolina was weak and getting weaker by the day.

The Secret War

There was a sort of secret war being waged in the South. As more and more patriots' homes and farms were destroyed, more and more southern colonists began to hate the British and their Loyalist supporters. The Southerners often kept these feelings to themselves or discussed them only with family. But burning inside many Southerners was a desire for revenge.

The ways Southerners sought revenge were not always heroic or even terribly noticeable. As Albert Marrin notes, it was not necessary to fire a gun to fight the enemy. "You might play stupid when a British officer asks you for directions, or give wrong directions, sending a patrol miles and hours out of its way. You might also help bridges collapse and trees fall 'accidently' across roads used by enemy supply columns."

But some southern people were fighting more aggressively against the British and their Loyalist supporters. These people were guerrilla fighters. They were untrained and organized themselves rather than submit to the authority of the Continental army. They were masters of trickery and sabotage.

Guerrillas worked in small groups ambushing enemies and destroying British equipment. They wore no uniforms and were quick to disappear if fired upon. Unlike regular army units that acquired and held territory, they simply attacked and disappeared. They were at home living in forests and caves. And because they were well known to local people, they always had friends they could trust to hide them or provide them with a meal.

The Swamp Fox

The most famous of these guerrilla fighters was a quiet, swarthy little man named Francis Marion. He was about fifty years old when the southern campaign was fought, although he moved like a boy. He and the members of his band dressed in greasy animal skins and many wore black leather hats. Marion never smiled, and one who knew him said "the man never said more than twenty words each day."

But Marion's actions spoke for him. He hated the British and Tories and the way they looted and burned the farms and homes of South Carolina. While he never felt he was cut out to be a "regular soldier," Marion made it his business to fight his own private war with the British and their supporters.

Marion made life miserable for Cornwallis and his troops, just when the general was trying to keep a firm hold on South Carolina so he could move north. Marion and his band of sixty or so raiders seemed to be a few steps behind the British, undoing what the redcoats thought they had accomplished.

After the battle of Camden, for instance, Cornwallis ordered 150 Continental prisoners to be escorted to a prison camp. They were accompanied by twenty-two Tory soldiers. Marion and sixteen of his men ambushed the procession and set the American prisoners free. Before the furious British soldiers could catch him, Marion disappeared into the Carolina swamps, an area he knew well.

Another time the British set out from their fort to go searching for Marion. They had a surprisingly clear trail to follow, but they just could not seem to catch up. Finally, they turned around to head back to their fort, only to find that Marion had burned it and their supplies to the ground.

Historians give a great deal of credit to Francis Marion for keeping the British from sweeping through the South into Virginia. Marion took shots at British troops on the march during the day. At night, when they were trying to rest, he and his men hid in nearby swamps and forests and made loud noises.

Francis Marion (center) at his makeshift camp in a southern swamp. Due to his aggressive guerrilla attacks against the British, Marion prevented the British from sweeping across the South.

Marion and his men cross the Pedee River in South Carolina to attack Tarleton's forces. Marion kept up a constant harassment of British troops, usually attacking at night when they were trying to sleep.

One British colonel was particularly upset by Marion's tactics. He wrote a letter to Cornwallis complaining that "they [Marion's men] will not sleep and fight like gentlemen, but like savages are eternally firing and whooping around us by night, and by day waylaying and popping at us from behind every tree."

Banastre Tarleton hated Marion. It offended him that Marion always seemed to get the best of him and his men. "He dares to laugh at us," said one of Butcher Tarleton's Tories, "and we do not like being the object of his merriment."

Tarleton was the one who gave Marion his nickname. He made it a point to keep searching for Marion, but in the end, the dark, mosquito-filled swamps proved too much for Tarleton. "He is a damned swamp fox," cursed Tarleton. "The devil himself couldn't catch him."

A Glimmer of Hope

In late spring 1781, Cornwallis was completely frustrated and impatient. Because of the success of Marion and other guerrilla fighters, he realized much of the South was too hard to hold. He wrote a letter to another officer announcing that he planned "to quit the Carolinas" and to move his army north to Virginia.

The British troops—over seventy-five hundred of them—spent the next two months moving north. They eventually set up headquarters in a small port on the York River on Chesapeake Bay in Virginia. The name of this port was Yorktown, and it would be the setting for the war's end.

George Washington, meanwhile, was keeping eternal watch over the British camped in New York City. The American camps were to the north and west of the city on hills high enough to give Washington a good look at any British movement.

Washington had been waiting, month after month, to have a chance to attack the British in New York. Finally, in the summer of 1781, it seemed that he might have his way. Washington heard news that a large French army of five thousand men had just landed in Newport, Rhode Island. They were on their way to Washington's camp and were eager to fight.

Washington was excited. He began making plans to defeat the British in New York City. He felt that he had enough manpower. The only thing he lacked was sea power. Washington hoped each day that he would hear news of a French fleet, which was supposed to be coming to New York Harbor to assist the Americans. If he could bottle up the British on land *and* sea, he knew he could end the war.

But Washington was disappointed. News reached him in August that the admiral of the French fleet, Francois Count de Grasse, was coming not to New York but to Chesapeake Bay. Washington was angry. He wrote in his journal, "I was obliged…to give up all idea of attacking New York."

Plan B

As Washington was fuming about his missed opportunity in New York City, five thousand French troops did indeed arrive in his camp. Washington took a second look at his plans and readjusted them. He had heard that Cornwallis and a large part of the British army were now in Yorktown. He could bottle Cornwallis up at Yorktown, since de Grasse was on his way to provide sea power. If he could not defeat the British under General Clinton in New York City, he would defeat them in Virginia.

The plan had large risks, however. After being encamped outside New York City for so long, Washington's departure would be suspicious. If General Clinton suspected what he was doing, he could send out his troops to catch Washington marching south to Virginia. If that happened, all might be lost.

Trickery saved the plan. Washington fooled General Clinton into thinking that he still intended to attack New York City. Washington left more than thirty-five hundred troops behind pretending to be keeping watch over the British in New York.

On August 25, Washington marched south with two thousand American troops and five thousand French. Continuing to fool the British, Washington ordered one flank of his army to swing around Staten Island in New York to give the appearance that he

A Driven Man

One of the most hated names of the Revolutionary War is that of Benedict Arnold. It is well known that he betrayed his country, that he was paid by the British to help them take over the American fortress at West Point. Interestingly, Arnold was one of the finest officers in Washington's army.

The problem, say historians, is that Arnold was a man who loved to spend money. He never seemed to have enough. He enjoyed a lavish house—far larger than other officers' homes—servants, and the best horses. He was also known for giving the most elegant dinner parties in Philadelphia.

One fellow officer who knew Arnold said, "Money is this man's god, and to get enough of it he would sacrifice his country."

Arnold and the head of British intelligence, John Andre, had worked out a detailed scheme. Arnold was to surrender West Point to British general Henry Clinton. However, the plan did not work. Andre himself was captured carrying messages from Arnold to Clinton, and West Point was safe.

Arnold, however, was never caught by the Americans. He joined the British army and was well paid for his service to them.

planned to surround the city. (At the last minute, these troops rushed west through New Jersey and continued their southward march.) Meanwhile, Washington and the rest of his men marched quickly toward Yorktown.

Troop movement was not the only way Washington deceived Clinton and the British. He let phony top-secret memos drift into the hands of men he suspected were Tories. He and his officers also asked Loyalists for directions—to places they had no intention of marching. He ordered huge bread-baking ovens to be built in New Jersey to create the impression that Americans were building a permanent camp for the French soldiers outside New York. All of these bits of misinformation led General Clinton to think he knew just what was happening. The British general and his men began preparing for the attack that would not come.

"Thoroughly and Openly Delighted"

It was not until Washington's troops marched through Philadelphia that General Clinton knew he had been tricked. But by then it was too late to catch them. Clinton did send a message to Cornwallis that Washington was coming, but there was little Cornwallis could do about it.

The only "if" in the attack was the arrival of de Grasse and the French fleet. If they were delayed, or if they were attacked by a British fleet, the land attack of the Americans would be no threat at all to Cornwallis.

The answer came in early September. Washington learned that the French fleet had arrived at Chesapeake Bay. All the pieces of the puzzle were in place.

The French who were with Washington were amazed at the change in him. Where days before he had been quiet and nervous, on hearing the news of the French fleet, he became jubilant. One French officer remarked, "I never saw a man more thoroughly and openly delighted than was General Washington at this moment."

Another officer agreed. "A child whose every wish had been granted could not have revealed a livelier emotion," he later wrote.

French general Rochambeau, who had marched a regiment of French troops to assist Washington, was crossing over by boat to Chester, where Washington was camped. Rochambeau had not yet heard the good news and was confused to see Washington waiting for him "dancing around on the dock, waving his hat." When Rochambeau stepped out of his boat, Washington grabbed him in a huge bear hug and danced him around the pier.

The news was even happier for Washington, for it was soon learned that de Grasse had brought twenty-five hundred more French troops who were eager to join the Americans in battle. It appeared that the Americans were in a fine position to defeat Cornwallis. "We have got him handsomely in a pudding bag," one American officer declared gleefully.

French general Rochambeau (above) assisted General Washington in the Revolutionary War. (Top) Rochambeau reviews the French troops brought over to fight alongside the patriots.

A New King George?

One would think that after the British surrendered at Yorktown, Americans would be proudly looking forward to their new independence. But that was not completely the case. There were troubles plaguing America in 1782, before the peace treaty was signed, that made many Americans nervous.

The Continental Congress was hampered by contention among its members. Each congressman had his own idea of how the new republic should be run. The cost of the war had added a strain to the budget. The colonies bickered over who should shoulder what percentage of the debt.

The squabbling led one army officer, Col. Lewis Nicola, to send a letter to General Washington. In his letter, Nicola said he believed a democratic republic would not work in America. He suggested a more traditional approach to the problem, and he said that his colleagues in the army agreed. The answer, according to them, was to establish a monarchy in America and to make Washington king.

Washington responded angrily in a letter to Nicola saying that "no occurrence in the course of the War, has given me more painful sensation than your information of there being such ideas existing in the Army."

Washington was confident that a republican government would work and urged Nicola "to banish these thoughts from your mind, and never communicate…a sentiment of the like nature."

When asked by Col. Lewis Nicola to become king, George Washington was appalled. He did not fight to free America from British rule only to accept an offer to rule a similar monarchy.

Yorktown by Siege

The Americans arrived in Yorktown in late September and dug trenches for themselves and their artillery. (The French had provided lots of cannons and heavy guns.) By October 9, the Americans were prepared to begin their attack. More than eighteen thousand French and American soldiers and sailors had the British surrounded.

Washington himself fired the first cannon. According to reports, the twenty-four-pound cannonball crashed into a house, where it killed a British general sitting at his dinner table.

Many of the British at Yorktown were living in homes which they had taken by force from American patriots. One home was that of Virginia governor Thomas Nelson, Jr., who was visiting the American and French lines. One French general asked Nelson if there was one good part of the town at which they should aim their cannons.

General Washington (left) fires the first cannon in the siege of Yorktown. (Below) The American siege of Yorktown.

Governor Nelson pointed immediately to a tall brick home. "Cornwallis may be there," he declared. "Have them fire there. It's my house."

Not surprisingly, the French and American gunners were reluctant to shoot cannons at the house. But Nelson insisted. In fact, he offered a cash reward to the first man who could score a direct hit on his house.

The bombardment of Yorktown was unceasing. Cornwallis knew that he could not escape, especially since a large fleet of French ships-of-the-line waited just offshore. He was trapped, and by October 17, he sent out a drummer and a white-flag bearer to surrender.

A New Nation

The defeat at Yorktown meant the end of the war. With more than one-third of the British army gone, there was no way the British could continue. Although skirmishes continued between Tories and settlers for more than a year on the frontier, the American Revolution was over.

The official terms of the war's end were worked out in Paris at a special series of meetings. On September 3, 1783, the Treaty of Paris was signed. The British troops and Loyalists evacuated the American shore, and the new nation was on its own.

Cornwallis surrenders to General Washington at Yorktown. The battle ended the Revolutionary War.

Washington met with his officers one last time. At the Fraunces Tavern on Pearl Street in New York City, a farewell luncheon was held on December 4, 1783. It was an emotional goodbye, as Benjamin Tallmadge, an American colonel who was there, remembered.

After pouring a glass of wine, Washington said, "With a heart full of love and gratitude, I now take leave of you. I most devoutly wish that your latter days may be as prosperous and happy as your former ones have been glorious and honorable."

All of the men were too choked up to speak, and Tallmadge recalled that Washington's voice cracked several times during his speech. He told them, "I cannot come to each of you, but shall feel obliged if each of you will come and take me by the hand."

One by one, the men came to Washington. He ignored their outstretched hands and gave each a hug and kiss. Wrote Tallmadge, "Such a scene of sorrow and weeping I had never before witnessed, and hope I may never be called upon to witness again…. Not a word was uttered to break the solemn silence…or to interrupt the tenderness of the…scene."

Washington said his final goodbyes and set off on his journey back to his home at Mount Vernon. The journey was no longer risky, for no enemy patrols were prowling. The new nation, filled with promise, had a great deal of growing to do.

And it was time to begin.

Cornwallis's surrender at Yorktown is front-page news in a colonial newspaper (above). (Above, left) The signing of the Treaty of Paris officially ends the Revolutionary War.

EPILOGUE

Survival?

In April 1783, Thomas Paine wrote, "The times that tried men's souls are over—and the greatest and completest revolution the world ever knew, gloriously and happily accomplished."

Six months later, as the last regiments of British redcoats sailed back to England, America rejoiced. Cannons boomed, crowds cheered, and people agreed with Paine's words. The hard times had come to an end. Victory had been seized, and America was a colony no more. No rules and restrictions from across the sea would bind Americans. They could trade with whomever they pleased. They were no longer banned from crossing the Alleghenies into the frontier; if they wanted to settle that new land, King George could not prohibit it.

But it could not have taken long for Americans to look around them and see that there were problems ahead. Physically, their new republic was in ruins. Large cities like Charleston and New York had been badly damaged in the fighting. Streets and roads were torn up, homes were gutted by fire, and rubbish lay in heaps everywhere.

The countryside was no better. The lush valleys and rolling hills of New York, Virginia, Pennsylvania, and New Jersey bore the scars of the war. Homes and barns had been destroyed by fire, and livestock had been killed by Loyalist and Indian raids. Farmers had been too busy during the war to pay attention to their land, and the fields were overgrown and neglected.

Washington, too, worried about the future of America.

I predict the worst consequences from a half-starved, limping government, always moving upon crutches and tottering at every step…. I do not conceive we can exist long as a nation without having lodged somewhere a power which will pervade the whole Union in as energetic a manner as the authority of the State governments extends over the several states.

Challenges to the Republic

The challenges faced by the new republic were varied. Some were domestic, like a huge war debt of $40 million, which forced Congress to impose heavy taxes on the American people. Others were more broad, involving Britain and other European nations. "Some of our problems threaten to devour us from within, and some from without," lamented a Pennsylvania merchant. "I do not know how we can survive such woes, only that we are surrounded by them."

Along the frontier, Native American tribes were still a threat to settlers. The Indians had remained loyal to the British, and most were intensely hostile toward Americans moving west. And the British continued to encourage the hostility by maintaining their outposts in the frontier.

Because of this, some Americans worried that the West could go up in flames again, and war would resume. John Jay, an American diplomat who helped negotiate the 1783 treaty between England and America, urged Congress to "keep America ready for war." The British outposts were, as Jay saw it, "pledges of enmity," or promises of continuing hatred, by the British government.

American diplomat John Jay worried that early America might find itself again at war—this time with American Indians. He encouraged America's leaders to remain prepared for war.

Trouble with the British

The American frontier was not the only place where the British posed a threat to the republic. British officials, still angry over their defeat in the Revolutionary War, directed their ships to harass American vessels on the high seas.

Sometimes the British seized entire ships, claiming the cargo as their own. More often, however, the British seized the strongest, ablest American sailors and forced them to sail British ships. This impressment, as it was called, was much feared by American sailors. Throughout the late 1700s and early 1800s, British ships impressed more than fifteen thousand American seamen.

The bad feelings between Britain and America were worsened as both sides failed to live up to the promises they had made in the 1783 treaty. Britain continued to control its outposts on the frontier, even though it had promised to abandon them. Americans who had seized property belonging to Loyalists

Alexander Hamilton worried about the future of the United States. He feared that the states would remain too separate and be unable to develop continental goals and loyalties.

refused to give the property up even though the treaty specified that such property had to be given back to Tories who returned to America after the war.

"It seems that we have as much fury toward [the British] as we did in 1775," wrote Boston lawyer Henry Webb in 1786. "They have no respect for our federation of states, perhaps we need to command more of it."

"A Half-Starved, Limping Government"

The process of rebuilding after war is extremely difficult under any circumstances. But it was even more difficult for the Americans. No strong central government existed that could direct the rebuilding. There was no agreement on how the country should be rebuilt. In spite of the new-found unity the colonies had attained to fight the British, they remained very separate. Each colony had its own idea of priorities and of how the new government should be run. "We were 13 separate colonies before, and today we are 13 separate free states," wrote a Massachusetts lawyer in 1784. "I hardly see that the difference exists from what we were to what we've become through the lean years of hardship."

Many of the leaders of the Revolutionary War were concerned about the lack of unity among the colonies. Alexander Hamilton, one of Washington's most trusted aides, urged Americans to begin to "think continentally." It was important, he said, for the power of the individual states to be pooled into a strong federal power.

Hamilton worried about a nation made up of "a number of petty states, with the appearance only of union, jarring jealous and perverse, without any determined direction, fluctuating and unhappy at home, weak and insignificant by their dissensions in the eyes of other nations."

It was true. The British had little or no respect for the new nation. Because of this, bad feelings between the two nations continued to grow. Benjamin Franklin recognized the overwhelming nature of America's problems when he said, "The War of the Revolution has been won, but the War of Independence is still to be fought."

That independence had not been won at Bunker Hill, Saratoga, or at Yorktown. It was still to be won in the coming years, and it had to be fought on other battlefields. Some would be military conflicts, others would be furious debates between the states on the nature of the new American nation.

The war of independence Benjamin Franklin had talked about would be different from other wars. It would need to be fought, and won, and fought again, by many different kinds of Americans.

For Further Reading

Elizabeth Anticaglia, *Heroines of '76*. New York: Walker and Co., 1975.

Genevieve Foster, *Year of Independence, 1776*. New York: Scribner's, 1970.

James C. Giblin, *Fireworks, Picnics, and Flags*. New York: Clarion Books, 1983.

Judith Berry Griffin, *Phoebe the Spy*. New York: Scholastic Books, 1977.

Robert Leckie, *The World Turned Upside Down*. New York: G. P. Putnam's Sons, 1973.

Ann McGovern, *The Secret Soldier*. New York: Four Winds Press, 1975.

Martin McPhillips, *The Battle of Trenton*. Morristown, NJ: Silver Burdett, 1985.

R. Conrad Stein, *The Story of Valley Forge*. Chicago: Children's Press, 1985.

C. Keith Wilbur, *Picture Book of the Revolution's Privateers*. Harrisburg, PA: Stackpole Books, 1973.

Works Consulted

Eric W. Barnes, *Free Men Must Stand*. New York: McGraw-Hill, 1962.

Fon W. Boardman, Jr., *Against the Iroquois*. New York: David McKay Co., 1978.

Clorinda Clark, *The American Revolution, 1775-83,* New York: McGraw-Hill, 1964.

R. Ernest Dupuy and Trevor N. Dupuy, *An Outline History of the American Revolution.* New York: Harper and Row, 1975.

L. Ethan Ellis, *40 Million Schoolbooks Can't Be Wrong*. New York: Macmillan, 1975.

Olga Hall-Quest, *From Colony to Nation*. New York: Dutton, 1966.

S. Carl Hirsch, *Famous American Revolutionary War Heroes*. Chicago: Rand McNally, 1974.

Zachary Kent, *The Surrender at Yorktown*. Chicago: Children's Press, 1989.

Bruce Lancaster, *The American Heritage History of the American Revolution.* New York: American Heritage Publishers, 1971.

Albert Marrin, *The War for Independence*. New York: Atheneum, 1988.

Milton Meltzer, *The American Revolutionaries: A History in Their Own Words*. New York: Thomas Y. Crowell, 1987.

Shirley Milgrim, *Haym Salomon, Liberty's Son*. New York: Jewish Publication Society, 1975.

Beatrice Siegel, *George and Martha Washington at Home in New York*. New York: Four Winds Press, 1989.

Alan Skeoch, *United Empire Loyalists and the American Revolution*. Toronto: Grolier, 1982.

Donald Sobol, *An American Revolutionary War Reader.* New York: Franklin Watts, 1964.

R. Conrad Stein, *The Story of the Boston Tea Party*. Chicago: Children's Press, 1984.

————, *The Story of Lexington and Concord*. Chicago: Children's Press, 1983.

Craig L. Symonds, *A Battlefield Atlas of the American Revolution*. Baltimore: Nautical and Aviation Publishing Co., 1986.

Index

Photo Credits

About the Author

Gail B. Stewart received her undergraduate degree from Gustavus Adolphus College in St. Peter, Minnesota. She did her graduate work in English, linguistics, and curriculum study at the College of St. Thomas and the University of Minnesota. Stewart taught English and reading for more than ten years.

She has written twenty-five books for young people, including a six-part series called *Living Spaces.* She has written several books for Lucent Books including *Drug Trafficking* and *Acid Rain.*

Stewart and her husband live in Minneapolis with their three sons, two dogs, and a cat. She enjoys reading (especially children's books) and playing tennis.